Water Use in Wisconsin, 2005

By Cheryl A. Buchwald

Open-File Report 2009–1076
Version 1.1, November 2011

U.S. Department of the Interior
U.S. Geological Survey

U.S. Department of the Interior
KEN SALAZAR, Secretary

U.S. Geological Survey
Suzette M. Kimball, Acting Director

U.S. Geological Survey, Reston, Virginia: 2009
Revised: November 2011

Suggested citation:
Buchwald, C.A., 2009, Water use in Wisconsin, 2005: U.S. Geological Survey Open-File Report 2009–1076, 74 p.

Contents

Figures

Tables

Conversion Factors and Abbreviations

Multiply	By	To Obtain
Length		
foot (ft)	0.3048	meter (m)
inch (in.)	2.54	centimeter (cm)
mile (mi)	1.609	kilometer (km)
Area		
acre	0.004047	square kilometer (km^2)
acre	0.001562	square mile (mi^2)
square mile (mi^2)	2.590	square kilometer (km^2)
Volume		
acre-foot (acre-ft)	1,233	cubic meter (m^3)
acre-foot (acre-ft)	325,851.43	gallon (gal)
gallon (gal)	0.003785	cubic meter (m^3)
gallon (gal)	3.785	liter (L)
million gallons (Mgal)	3,785.00	cubic meter (m^3)
Flow rate		
acre-foot per day (acre-ft/d)	325,851.43	gallon per day (gal/d)
cubic foot per second (ft^3/s)	0.02832	cubic meter per second (m^3/s)
gallon per day (gal/d)	0.003785	cubic meter per day (m^3/d)
gallon per day per acre [(gal/d)/acre]	1.069	cubic meter per day per square kilometer [$(m^3/d)/km^2$]
gallon per minute (gal/min)	0.06309	liter per second (L/s)
inch per year (in/yr)	25.4	millimeter per year (mm/yr)
million gallons per day (Mgal/d)	133,680.56	cubic foot per day (ft^3/d)
million gallons per day (Mgal/d)	0.04381	cubic meter per second (m^3/s)
million gallons per year (Mgal/yr)	0.002738	million gallons per day (Mgal/d)
Energy		
gigawatthour (gWh)	3,600,000,000,000	joule (J)
kilowatthour (kWh)	3,600,000	joule (J)

Additional abbreviations used in this report

AWUDS	Aggregate water-use data system
DATCP	Wisconsin Department of Agriculture, Trade and Consumer Protection
DOA	Wisconsin Department of Administration
DOE	U.S. Department of Energy
EPA	U.S. Environmental Protection Agency
GRN	Groundwater Retrieval Network and High Capacity Well Database
HUC	Hydrologic Unit Code
MNDNR	Minnesota Department of Natural Resources
MNDNR WAPP	Minnesota Department of Natural Resources Water Appropriations Permit Program
MRLC	Multi-Resolution Land Characteristics Consortium
NASS	National Agricultural Statistics Service
NLCD	National Land Cover Database
NRC	National Research Council
NRCS	Natural Resources Conservation Service
NWIS	National Water Information System
NWUIP	National Water-Use Information Program
PSC	Public Service Commission of Wisconsin
SIC	Standard Industrial Classification
SDWIS	Safe Drinking Water Information System
SWUDS	Site-specific water-use data system
US Census	U.S. Census Bureau
USDA	U.S. Department of Agriculture
USGS	U.S. Geological Survey
WBD	Watershed Boundary Dataset
WDNR	Wisconsin Department of Natural Resources
WI WSC	Wisconsin Water Science Center
Wis. Admin. Code NR	Wisconsin Administrative Code, Natural Resources Chapter

Million gallons per day (Mgal/d)

This report converts annual volumes of water into average daily quantities in million gallons per day (Mgal/d), because annual volumes of water often involve large numbers. To help visualize this amount, one million gallons would form a cube that is approximately 51 feet on each side.

To put water use in perspective, the typical person may use 2 to 7 gallons to flush a toilet, 25 to 50 gallons to take an average 5-minute shower, or use 9 to 12 gallons to wash dishes with an automatic dishwasher or 20 gallons to wash dishes by hand (U.S. Environmental Protection Agency, 1995).

Some typical Wisconsin industries may use 1,500 gallons to process 1 barrel of beer, 1,360 gallons to make 1 ton of cement, 9.3 gallons to process one can of fruit or vegetables, or 5.4 gallons to make 1 board foot of lumber (U.S. Environmental Protection Agency, 1995).

Water Use in Wisconsin, 2005

By Cheryl A. Buchwald

Abstract

The U.S. Geological Survey (USGS) Wisconsin Water Science Center is responsible for presenting data collected or estimated for water withdrawals and diversions every 5 years to the National Water-Use Information Program (NWUIP). This program serves many purposes such as quantifying how much, where, and for what purpose water is used; tracking and documenting water-use trends and changes; and providing these data to other agencies to support hydrologic projects. In 2005, data at both the county and subbasin levels were compiled into the USGS national water-use database system; these data are published in a statewide summary report and a national circular. This publication, Water Use in Wisconsin, 2005, presents the water-use estimates for 2005; this publication also describes how these water-use data were determined (including assumptions used), limitations of using these data, and trends in water-use data presented to the NWUIP.

Estimates of water use in Wisconsin indicate that about 8,608 million gallons per day (Mgal/d) were withdrawn during 2005. Of this amount, about 7,622 Mgal/d (89 percent) were from surface-water sources and about 986 Mgal/d (11 percent) were from ground-water sources. Surface water used for cooling at thermoelectric-power plants constituted the largest portion of daily use at 6,898 Mgal/d. Water provided by public-supply water utilities is the second largest use of water and totaled 552 Mgal/d. Public supply served approximately 71 percent of the estimated 2005 Wisconsin population of 5.54 million people; two counties—Milwaukee and Dane—accounted for more than one-third of the public-supply withdrawal. Industrial and irrigation were the next major water uses at 471 and 402 Mgal/d, respectively. Non-irrigational agricultural (livestock and aquaculture) accounted for approximately 155 Mgal/d and is similar to the combined withdrawal for the remaining water-use categories of domestic, commercial, and mining (131 Mgal/d).

Data on water use in Wisconsin by source of water and category of use have been compiled at 5-year intervals since 1950. During the past 55 years (1950–2005), water withdrawn to meet demands for public supply and self-supplied irrigation, industrial, commercial, domestic, and livestock increased 333 percent (1,117 Mgal/d). The greatest increases were for public supply, industrial, and irrigation, and are reflected in the increasing total per-capita water-use values. In recent (2000 and 2005) water-use estimation years, both public-supply and self-supplied domestic per-capita-use values have been declining. This can be attributed, at least in part, to a reduction in industrial-water deliveries, increased water-efficiency standards, and the implementation of leak-detection programs and water-conservation practices. However, when making comparisons to evaluate trends among other Wisconsin water-use estimation years, it is important to be aware of changes that may have occurred in estimation methods or objectives that create differences. Some changes that have occurred are the availability of data and information about water use, changes in data sources and estimation methods, and the inclusion and exclusion of certain water-use categories. These differences may have an effect on apparent trends and make comparing trends difficult.

Introduction

Wisconsin encompasses more than 56,000 mi^2, of which 15 percent is covered by water (Wisconsin Department of Natural Resources, 1998; Multi-Resolution Land Characteristics Consortium, 2001). The State has three principal aquifer systems (Olcott, 1992), more than 15,000 lakes, 32,000 mi of rivers and streams (Wisconsin Department of Natural Resources, 2008a, 2008b), and borders two Great Lakes—Lake Michigan and Lake Superior. The abundant water resources have been important to the settlement (that is, community formation) of Wisconsin and the development of its agricultural and industrial livelihoods; however, this development can and has affected future water availability in parts of the State as seen by declining water levels and reductions in water quality. This has led to recent legislative activity resulting in the creation of ground-water protection areas and the establishment of two ground-water management areas in which the Wisconsin Department of Natural Resources (WDNR) is mandated under Wisconsin Administrative Rules (Chapter NR 820) to protect and manage ground-water resources (Wisconsin State Legislature, 2007). The U.S. Geological Survey (USGS) Wisconsin Water-Use Information Program has a critical role in assessing how, where, and in what quantity water is used. By better understanding water use in Wisconsin, the USGS can assist State and local agencies to meet current and future demands as well as assist in sustaining these water resources.

Data on water use in Wisconsin were first compiled for the year 1950; since then, water-use data have been compiled for every fifth year. The specific calendar year (1950, 1955, 1960, etc.) for which these water-use data were collected and estimated is referred to in this report as a compilation, or because these data are collected on a 5-year interval (not to be confused with 5 years of data), it may also be referred to in this report as a 5-year compilation. This report, "Water use in Wisconsin, 2005," marks the sixth in such titled series (others include 1979, 1985, 1990, 1995, and 2000). Water use in the broadest sense, and as defined for this 2005 compilation, is the amount of water conveyed to a place for various types of use; this also is defined by the USGS handbook for collecting water-use data as off-stream water use (U.S. Geological Survey, 2008a). Wisconsin's water may be diverted from surface-water sources (rivers and lakes) or withdrawn from ground-water sources (water-bearing formations below land surface also known as an aquifer). In this report, springs are considered surface-water features while water flowing from artesian wells is considered ground water from an aquifer system. When water is withdrawn, it either may be removed from the immediate water environment (consumptive use) or be returned to a water source (return flow); in either case there is possible water loss in transit (conveyance loss). This 2005 compilation does not consider in-stream water uses, which is water that is neither diverted nor withdrawn, but is used in place to meet certain human, ecological, or environmental needs, such as for hydroelectric-power generation; waste assimilation; or preservation of fish, wildlife, and wetlands (U.S. Geological Survey, 2008a).

Eight categories of water use in Wisconsin in 2005 are described— public supply, domestic, irrigation, non-irrigational agriculture (which includes subcategories for livestock and aquaculture), industrial, commercial, thermoelectric power, and mining. Water use often is a component of a county- or subbasin plan for managing water resources; therefore, for each water-use category, withdrawals were compiled by water source (surface water or ground water), political boundaries (by county), and geographical boundaries (by subbasin)[1].

These water-use data are collected by the USGS Wisconsin Water Science Center (WI WSC) to serve the National Water-Use Information Program (NWUIP), which is part of the National Water Information System (NWIS), to provide science-based information on the Nation's water resources (U.S. Geological Survey, 2008b). The USGS NWUIP has compiled and published water-use information and data since 1950 (MacKichan, 1951, 1957; MacKichan and Kammerer, 1961; Murray, 1968; Murray and Reeves, 1972, 1977; Solley and others, 1983, 1988, 1993, 1998; Hutson and others, 2004). This program serves many purposes such as quantifying how much and where water is used, tracking and documenting water-use changes, and providing these data to other agencies to support hydrologic projects. Data for every

fifth year, as described previously, at county and subbasin levels are compiled into a national water-use database system; these data are published in a statewide summary report and a national circular. These data and reports, along with later revisions, can be accessed through the Wisconsin water-use data page at http://wi.water.usgs.gov/data/wateruse html (U.S. Geological Survey, 2008c). This USGS series of water-use reports serves as one of the few sources of information about regional or national trends in water use (Hutson and others, 2004).

Quantifying the amount of water used, and where and how it is used, is essential for water-resources scientists, planners, and managers for such reasons as to:

- Determine the effect on hydrologic systems; in other words, there is a connection between water use and water quantity, water flow, and water quality

- Evaluate water resources and future water availability

- Improve our understanding of the factors that affect water use

- Establish which data are needed to make informed decisions and for better planning

- Assess consumptive water use

- Identify trends to guide preservation or development of the water resources or to show where it may be possible to improve water-use efficiency

- Improve ability to forecast future demands

- Evaluate how water use is linked with economic activity

In fact, as a result of the 2002 Waters of Wisconsin Forum under the Conserve Wisconsin agenda, Governor Doyle introduced, in 2003, a broad package of legislation and executive orders to help protect the waters of Wisconsin. Information about water use, in particular ground-water use, was recognized as a necessary component for protecting against the depletion of Wisconsin's ground-water resources. The 2003 Wisconsin Act 310 requires the WDNR to collect data and information with respect to high-capacity ground-water use (Wisconsin State Legislature, 2004, 2007). It is expected that these developments will foster increased collaboration between the USGS WI WSC, the WDNR, other State and local agencies, other USGS water-use specialists, agricultural growers associations, and other organizations to continually improve the water-use estimates in future studies.

Purpose and Scope

This report describes the USGS WI WSC water-use compilation methods and water use in Wisconsin for 2005. It provides descriptions of each water-use category and presents data collected and estimates for surface- and ground-water

---

[1]To learn more about delineating hydrologic units, refer to U.S. Department of Agriculture (2004).

withdrawals that were summarized and submitted to the NWUIP. Water-use data are presented in county-level tables throughout the body of the report, and the water-use data for subbasins are provided in the appendixes at the end of the report. The report also describes assumptions and limitations inherent to the estimation approach used and water-use trends in Wisconsin from 1950 to 2005.

There were several specific objectives of the 2005 Wisconsin water-use compilation. The 2005 compilation effort sought to re-evaluate estimation approaches that were applied in past compilations; previous water-use coefficients were either verified or updated. "Master Lists" for municipal pubic-supply water facilities, self-supplied industries, commercial businesses, and aquacultural facilities were redeveloped to collect the most recent data or identify additional sites of water use. Water-use estimates by subbasin and for commercial and mining water-use categories were reinstated. This 2005 water use in Wisconsin publication also has been expanded compared to reports of previous compilation years to provide more data and information about water use, data sources, and estimation methods.

Overview of the Wisconsin Water-Use Compilations

Around 1950, the USGS (at that time called the "Geological Survey") began compiling water-use data every 5 years at the State level and producing a series of reports ("Water-Supply Papers"), which contained information about source, availability, use, and quality of water for particular population centers or regions of Wisconsin; these reports typically were a guide for suitability planning of community public-water supplies. Wisconsin water-use data for the years of 1950, 1955, 1960, 1965, 1970, and 1975 were published in the National water-use reports by MacKichan (1951, 1957), MacKichan and Kammerer (1961), Murray (1968), and Murray and Reeves (1972, 1977). In 1977, the U.S. Congress established the NWUIP to collect data at a local level (e.g., by county). In 1978, the USGS in Wisconsin (at that time called the "U.S. Department of Interior Geological Survey") entered into a cooperative agreement with the WDNR to inventory water use in Wisconsin as part of the Regional Aquifer-System Analysis (RASA) Program Northern Midwest study area (Sun and others, 1997). As a result, the first report of "Water Use in Wisconsin" was published in 1982 for the year 1979 (Lawrence and Ellefson, 1982). Other published studies soon followed in the 1980s (Lawrence and others, 1984; Krohelski and others, 1987). During this time, the NWUIP created two USGS internal databases—site-specific water-use data system (SWUDS) and aggregate water-use data system (AWUDS). SWUDS stores measurements and estimates of water use by individual users. AWUDS stores aggregated estimates of water use by county, subbasin, and aquifer system. The AWUDS database, first used in 1985, is specifically designed to store

and handle the aggregate water-use information compiled for the USGS (5-year) Wisconsin water-use reports, including Ellefson and others (1987, 1993, 1997, and 2002). In late 2004, the NWUIP released a new version of the SWUDS database to its Water Science Centers. Currently (2009), the WI WSC is reviewing its former data archives and is preparing to transfer these data along with new site-specific water-use data that were collected or estimated, since last used in 1994, into the new GUI-based version.

Changes for the 2005 Report

The overall aim of water-use science is to first compile the best data available and second, to purposefully estimate the largest water-use categories. Water-use terminology has changed during the course of USGS 5-year compilations (1950–2000) as described in the glossary available at http://pubs.usgs.gov/circ/2004/circ1268/htdocs/text-glossary.html (U.S. Geological Survey, 2008d). In addition, there have been shifts away from producing estimates where data are sparse or unreliable. A compilation matrix provided in table 1 and the following text will briefly summarize shifts between water-use report years.

An estimate of water use is complicated when data are sparse or of poor quality. This results in estimates that have high uncertainty. NWUIP made some water-use data elements optional, to be included by States that may have better data available (e.g., Arkansas and Indiana) and to require only off-stream water-use estimates for future compilations. Therefore, the categories of mining, commercial, wastewater treatment, reservoir evaporation, reclaimed water, and hydroelectricity were added for a few compilations and then discontinued for the Nation, after 1995, although mining and commercial (optional for Wisconsin) water uses were reinstated in 2005. In 2000, water-use estimates were not compiled by subbasin, nor were consumptive-use data collected for any of the categories, and public-supply delivery data were not collected. Additionally, Wisconsin water-use summaries prior to 1990 did not include aquaculture, and summaries prior to 2000 only included an estimate for crop irrigation. In 2000, estimates for golf course irrigation were electively added; in 2005, estimates for commercial, thermoelectric power at non-public power utilities, and other irrigation were electively added. Also in 2005, the WI WSC reinstated public-supply delivery data and for livestock water use added a few additional livestock types and updated a few livestock animal water-use coefficients; the NWUIP provided an estimate for the State's mining water-use category. Water use by aquifer system became an AWUDS aggregation level in 1985, but was deemed optional for Wisconsin; however, it is currently (2009) provided as a generalized estimate through limited analysis. It is expected that 2005 water-use data will be analyzed by aquifer system prior to the 2010 compilation.

Table 1. U.S. Geological Survey compilation matrix for Wisconsin water-use estimation, 1950 – 2005. A compilation is defined as a specific calendar year for which water-use data have been compiled.

[x, complete estimate; c, consumptive water use was estimated; p, partial estimate; --, not estimated; thermoelectric power, thermoelectric-power generation]

	Aggregation level				Water-use categories														
					Publicly supplied		Self supplied												
					Public supply									Non-irrigational agriculture		Irrigation		
Year	State	County	8-digit HUC	Aquifer	Total	By delivery	Domestic	Industrial	Commercial	Thermoelectric power	Hydro-electric power	Wastewater treatment[1]	Mining	Livestock	Aquaculture	Agricultural	Golf courses	Other
2005	x	x	x	--	x	x	x	x	x	x	--	--	x	xc	xc	x	x	x
2000	x	x	--	p	x	--	x	x	--	--	--	--	--	xc	xc	x	x	--
1995	x	x	x	p	x	x	xc	xc	xc	xc	x	x	pc	xc	pc	xc	--	--
1990	x	x	x	p	x	x	xc	xc	xc	xc	x	x	pc	xc	pc	xc	--	--
1985	x	x	x	p	x	x	xc	xc	xc	xc	x	x	--	xc	--	xc	--	--
1979	x	x	--	--	x	x	x	x	--	x	x	--	--	x	--	x	--	--
1975	x	--	--	--	x	--	x	x	--	x	x	--	--	x	--	x	--	--
1970	x	--	--	--	x	--	x	x	--	x	x	--	--	x	--	x	--	--
1965	x	--	--	--	x	--	x	x	--	x	x	--	--	x	--	x	--	--
1960	x	--	--	--	x	--	x	x	--	x	x	--	--	x	--	x	--	--
1955	x	--	--	--	x	--	x	x	--	x	x	--	--	x	--	x	--	--
1950	x	--	--	--	x	--	x	x	--	x	x	--	--	x	--	x	--	--

[1] Wastewater treatment includes an estimate for the number of public facilities and return flow but excludes reclaimed wastewater.

= Compilation structure or category definition changed

= Estimation method modified or changed from previous compilation year

= Coefficient changed from previous compilation year

Data Collection and Methods of Analysis

During this study, data and information from a variety of sources were collected, analyzed, and interpreted. Data collection was done by USGS during 2006–2007 and largely come from the WDNR, U.S. Department of Agriculture (USDA), U.S. Department of Energy (DOE), Public Service Commission of Wisconsin (PSC), U.S. Environmental Protection Agency (USEPA), and USGS. The only primary water-use data collected by the USGS specific to this compilation effort was for aquaculture. As of 2005, water-use data were reported only for municipal wells as part of the permit requirements (Wisconsin Administrative Code (Wis. Admin. Code) NR 820.13). Limited surface-water withdrawal data were collected by the WDNR, mainly for paper mills and publicly owned power-generation plants. The data acquired for this compilation are for 2005 or are from an acquisition year that is closest to it. Specific sources of data are further discussed under the related water-use category. Each 5-year compilation is an attempt to incorporate data from the above-listed sources with water-use category-specific methods to produce water-use estimates primarily at the county level. Seven of the eight water-use categories were prepared by the WI WSC. Summary data were compiled by combining actual and estimated values; site-specific information was used when available. Throughout the report there are comparisons to former compilations (in particular, the 2000 dataset); those data, which are archived in AWUDS, can be obtained from the USGS National Water-Use website at http://water.usgs.gov/watuse/ (U.S. Geological Survey, 2008c). Additional information about this study along with summaries of, and access to, data that have been revised since originally published, can be found at the following website: http://wi.water.usgs.gov/data/wateruse.html.

A "Master List" is a basic tool for compiling water-use data (Hutson, 2007); a "Master List" often links the name of a facility to ancillary information gathered in separate data-collection efforts. In 2005, only public-supply water use was required to be reported for the State; therefore, a "Master List" of municipal public-supply water utilities was possible. None of the self-supplied water-use categories were required to report water use. Complete "Master Lists" of self-supplied users were not possible (e.g., domestic use); however, for most water-use categories partial site lists were possible, especially for larger water users within the industrial, commercial, and irrigation categories where a high-capacity ground-water well approval or surface-water withdrawal or diversion permit was sought from the WDNR (although the source information may be outdated, incomplete, or erroneous). Approvals or permits are required for (1) a ground-water well that is capable of withdrawing more than 70 gal/min or for any wells on a single property if the combined pumping capacity of all wells is at least 100,000 gal/d (Wis. Admin. Code NR 812.07(53)); (2) a surface-water diversion that is greater than 2 Mgal/d (Section s. 281.35, Wis. Stats.); (3) a surface-water withdrawal for agricultural or golf course irrigation (independent of any minimum withdrawal) (Section s. 30.18, Wis. Stats.); and (4) water withdrawals with a consumptive loss of more than 2 Mgal/d (Wis. Admin. Code NR 142) (Wisconsin State Legislature, 2000, 2006). An approval or permit (prior to 2007) does not mean that reporting of water use was required; therefore, all self-supplied water-use categories are estimated. An early history about water permitting in Wisconsin was written by Schmid (1961). As of 2003, a couple of helpful summaries about Wisconsin's ground-water withdrawal laws, including reporting of water use, were prepared by the WDNR (Wisconsin Department of Natural Resources, 1997) and Wisconsin Department of Justice (Dawson, 2003), and by 2009, a report by the Wisconsin Groundwater Coordinating Council (2007).

Methods of water-use estimation varied among water-use categories, and sometimes a mix of methods were applied in each category to derive a final estimate. The central water-use estimation methods included using coefficients, past reported data, recently collected data, or default water-use values. Although water-use estimates for mining, livestock, and aquaculture were provided by the NWUIP, only water-use data for mining were used for the 2005 Wisconsin compilation because more specific data and information were obtained for livestock and aquacultural water uses.

Data in this report are categorized into 8 water-use categories, 2 water sources, 72 counties, and 52 subbasins (also known as an 8-digit hydrologic unit or a cataloging unit; see also the Federal Standards for Delineation of Hydrologic Unit Boundaries for more information about watershed delineation (U.S. Department of Agriculture, 2004)). The water-use data in this report are average daily quantities used in million gallons per day (Mgal/d). Seasonal water use for irrigation and particular commercial water uses (e.g., schools and campgrounds) have been averaged for the year to compare with annual values from the other water-use categories; therefore, the rate of withdrawal would be greater during the period of actual use. All population and water-use numerical data are rounded to a minimum of three significant figures. Because values are rounded independently, the sums of individually rounded numbers may not equal the totals. All water-use data compiled for this report are stored in AWUDS and are available by both county and subbasin on the World Wide Web at http://water.usgs.gov/watuse/wudata.html.

Population Data

Water use is related to population density (population per unit area) and population growth (positive or negative change in population over time). Other demographic data such as age, income distribution, and household size can be obtained to further explore water use with respect to the characteristics of the population. In this compilation, population data were used to determine how many persons are provided water from a water utility or are self-supporting, to calculate per-capita water-use statistics, and to track trends in population redistribution. Population and population density data for Wisconsin in 2005 by county and subbasin are provided in appendix 1a and 1b. The population density values listed describe the number of people per unit of land area (square mile); therefore, the amount of land covered by water is not considered in the calculation. The population of Wisconsin in 2005 is estimated by the U.S. Census Bureau to be 5.54 million (2006), which is a gain of more than 172,500 persons (or 3.17 percent) since the 2000 population census. Counties with growth of more than 10,000 persons since 2000 are (in increasing order)—Outagamie, Kenosha, Brown, St. Croix, Waukesha, and Dane (fig. 1). The fastest growing counties with growth exceeding 10 percent are Adams (11.7 percent) and St. Croix (22.1 percent). No county is substantially losing population; although, in Milwaukee, there was a loss of approximately 18,500 persons (-1.97 percent). The least populated counties are located in far northern Wisconsin, which also has the lowest population density. The most densely populated counties within the State are Milwaukee, Waukesha, Racine, and Kenosha (appendix 1a). In fact, just over one-third (or 37.6 percent) of the State's population lives in southeastern Wisconsin's eight counties, using southeastern Wisconsin as defined by WDNR Regions (fig. 1) (Wisconsin Department of Natural Resources, 2008a). About one-half of Wisconsin residents live within the Great Lakes Basin, while the other half live within the Mississippi River Basin (appendix 1b). The most densely populated subbasins are Pike-Root Rivers and Milwaukee River in southeastern Wisconsin, covering the Milwaukee metropolitan area (fig. 2).

The 2005 population by county dataset originated from the Population Division of the U.S. Census Bureau (U.S. Census Bureau, 2006) and was provided by the NWUIP for the WI WSC; the 2005 population by subbasin data also were provided by the NWUIP. There were a few revisions to the national dataset to accommodate the most significant modifications of the 1:250,000-scale coverage of hydrologic unit (referred to as HUC250) boundaries for Wisconsin; these modifications are part of the new Wisconsin Watershed Boundary Dataset available at http://datagateway nrcs.usda.gov/GatewayHome.html. Community-level population data for 2005 were obtained from the Wisconsin Department of Administration (DOA) (Wisconsin Department of Administration–Demographic Services Center, 2006); however, only the decennial years contained U.S. Census data so the projected 2005 data could not be directly used and needed to be adjusted to equal the county-level U.S. Census population for 2005.

Per-Capita Water Use

Per-capita use or water use on a per person basis is often taken as an indication of the lifestyle of a resident population but it also may be used to track water conservation or the lack thereof. Additionally, per-capita use can be applied to estimate future water use or needs. Several factors may affect per-capita water use, such as climate, water rates, demographics, amount of public use and loss, and scale of industrial or commercial activity. Per-capita use was estimated for total water use in Wisconsin by water-use category and water source (table 2), for county-level water use by water-use purpose and water source (table 3), and is provided in table 4. In 2005, the average per-capita use, including thermoelectric-power generation water use, was 1,554.9 gal/d per person; excluding thermoelectric-power generation water use, it was 308.9 gal/d per person. This is compared to the 2000 compilation (Ellefson and others, 2002), which was determined to be 1,422.0 and 285.7 gal/d per person, respectively. The per-capita use for surface water remained nearly unchanged, while the per-capita use for ground water increased slightly from 154.9 gal/d per person in 2000 to 177.5 gal/d per person in 2005, largely attributed to the increased estimation of irrigation water use. This report also provides additional information about per-capita use in the sections for public-supply and self-supplied domestic water use.

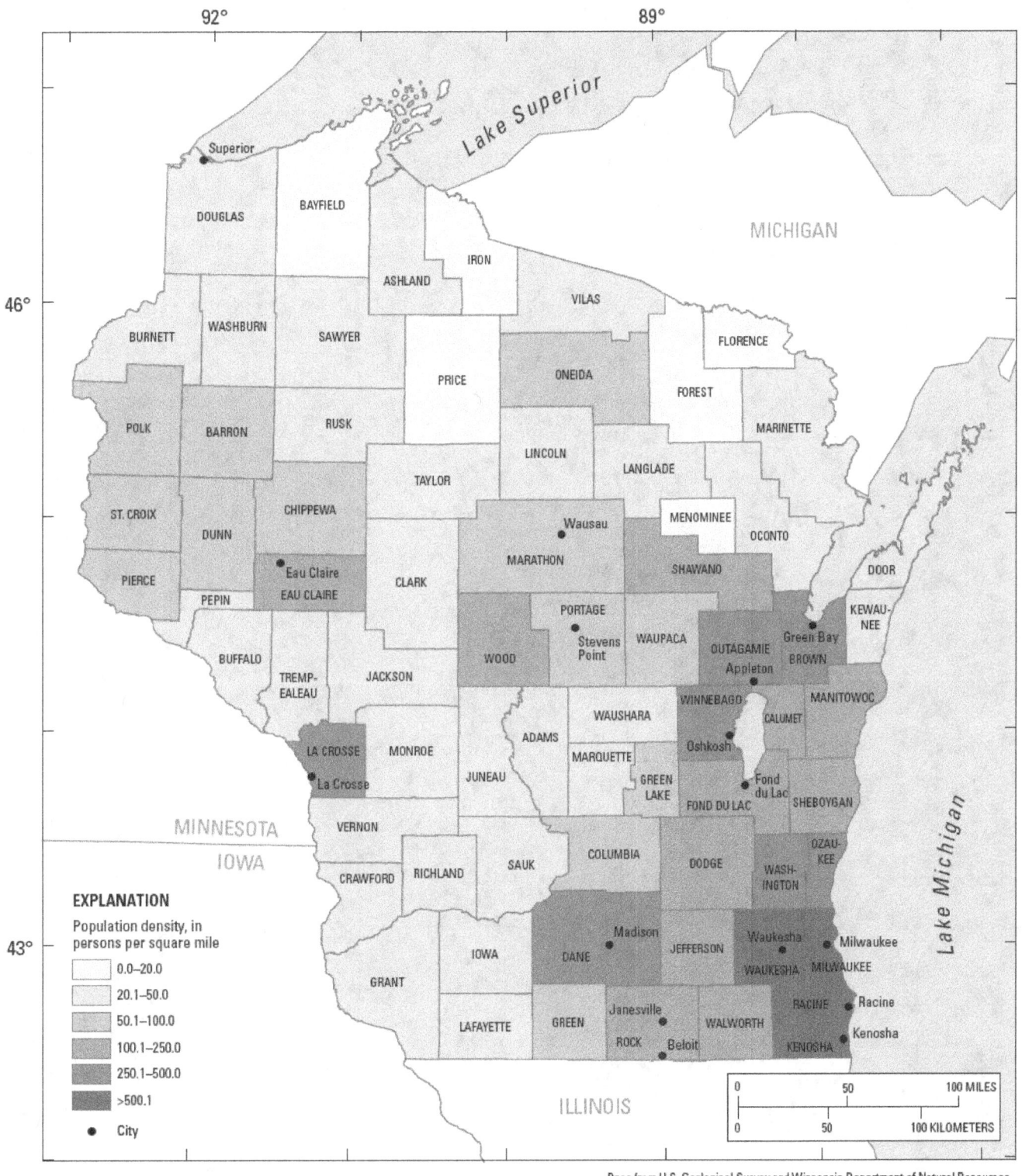

Figure 1.   Counties, select population centers, and estimated population density in Wisconsin, 2005.

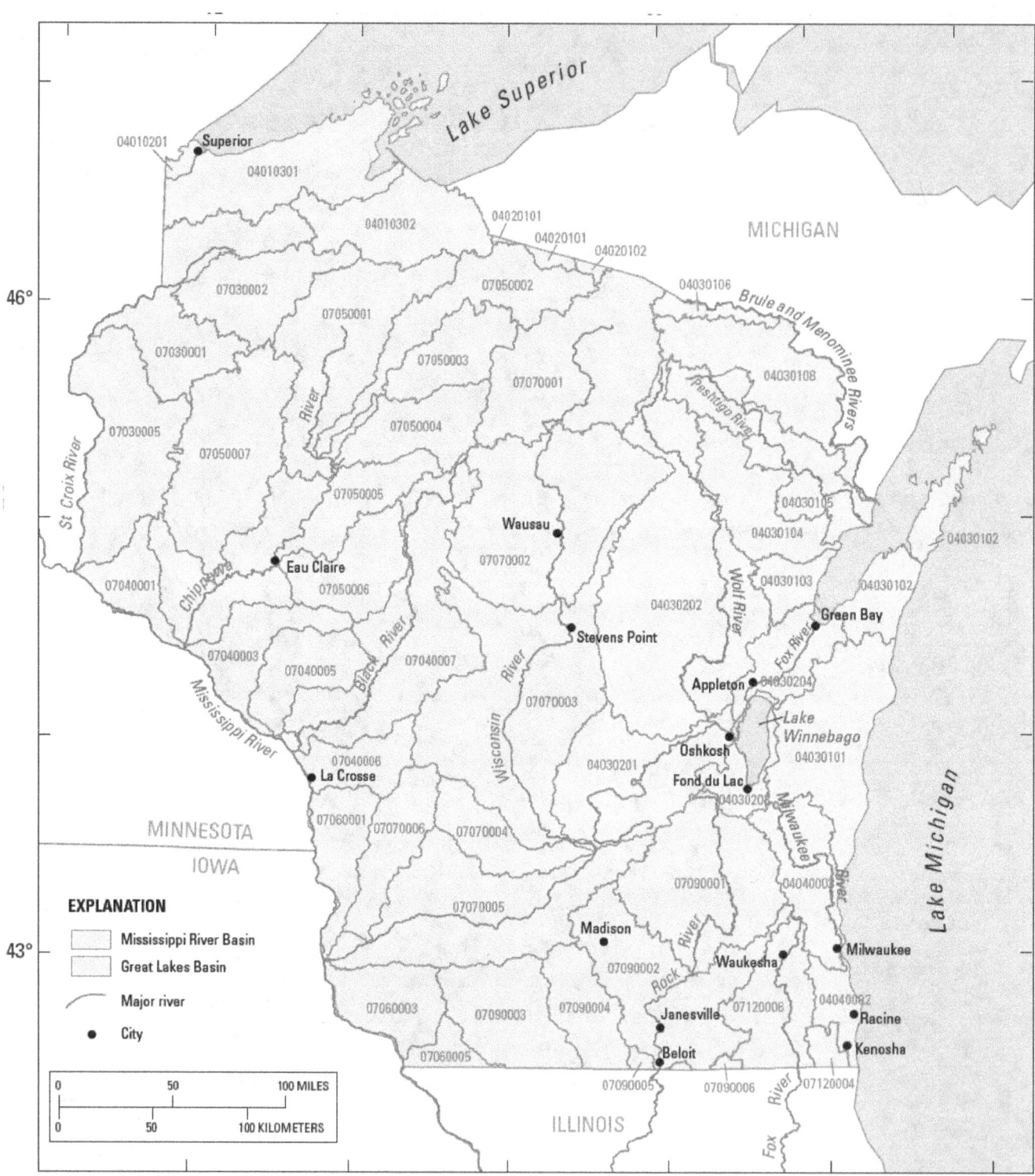

Figure 2. Subbasins and major hydrologic features of Wisconsin. (The 8-digit hydrologic unit codes shown on this map correspond with subbasin names listed in appendix 1b.)

Table 2. Wisconsin total water use by water source and by category, 2005.

[Mgal/d, million gallons per day; thermoelectric-power generation water-use category has been abbreviated to thermoelectric]

WITHDRAWALS by water-use category, in Mgal/d[a]

Water source	Publicly supplied	Self supplied									By source		By source, excluding thermoelectric	
	Public supply	Domestic	Irrigation[b]	Non-irrigational agriculture		Industrial	Commercial	Thermo-electric	Mining		Total	Percent of total	Total	Percent of total
				Livestock	Aquaculture									
Ground water	305.42	87.32	386.57	65.57	38.48	70.93	10.66	3.37	17.59		985.91	11.5	982.54	57.5
Surface water	246.97	.00	15.22	7.27	43.24	399.96	.00	6,894.56	14.93		7,622.15	88.5	727.59	42.5
Total	552.39	87.32	401.79	72.84	81.72	470.89	10.66	6,897.93	32.52		8,608.06	100	1,710.13	100

[a] As of 2005, none of the self-supplied water-use categories were required to report use to the Wisconsin Department of Natural Resouces, and as a result, confidence is less in these water-use estimates than those that are publicly supplied.

[b] The 2005 irrigation estimate (in particular, for ground water) is believed to be at the higher end of the range of possible irrigation water use. Irrigation water use is expected to be refined for the 2010 compilation to better reflect the irrigation variables of each county, such as crop type, soil type, topography, and climate.

Table 3.   Wisconsin water use by water-use purpose, water source, and county, 2005.

[Mgal/d, Million gallons per day, Thermoelectric, thermoelectric power generation]

| County | WITHDRAWALS, in Mgal/d | | | | | | | | | | | |
| | By water-use purpose[a] | | | | | | | | | By water source | | |
	Domestic	Livestock	Aqua-culture	Irrigation	Industrial	Commercial	Thermo-electric	Mining	Public use and loss[b]	Ground water	Surface water	Total
Adams	1.06	0.18	0.08	44.15	0.18	0.28	0.00	0.00	0.09	45.94	0.08	46.02
Ashland	.66	.14	.60	.07	2.53	.27	50.56	.04	.28	.82	54.33	55.15
Barron	2.19	1.60	.04	10.36	3.44	.55	.00	.25	1.18	19.11	.50	19.61
Bayfield	.61	.21	11.47	.17	.24	.20	.00	.88	.15	6.07	7.86	13.93
Brown	11.50	2.22	.04	.91	79.18	6.69	413.38	.78	5.40	21.07	499.03	520.10
Buffalo	.65	1.44	.00	2.34	.41	.09	533.16	.00	.16	5.49	532.76	538.25
Burnett	.75	.23	.77	.40	.07	.13	.00	.15	.08	2.07	.51	2.58
Calumet	1.99	1.20	.00	.35	2.26	.63	.00	.01	.90	5.34	2.00	7.34
Chippewa	1.34	1.76	.00	3.29	6.93	1.09	.00	.57	1.01	11.67	4.32	15.99
Clark	1.38	3.12	.04	.54	.51	.19	.00	.38	.36	5.52	1.00	6.52
Columbia	2.97	1.11	.28	1.72	2.26	.96	18.50	.34	.22	10.02	18.34	28.36
Crawford	1.13	.74	.00	.31	.80	.37	.00	.06	.30	3.32	.39	3.71
Dane	30.46	2.79	2.14	6.16	5.31	13.94	226.69	1.60	9.36	69.11	229.34	298.45
Dodge	4.05	2.39	.00	.64	3.43	.91	1.97	.63	1.59	12.91	2.70	15.61
Door	1.55	.48	2.16	1.10	.35	.57	.00	.25	.44	4.90	2.00	6.90
Douglas	3.56	.12	3.51	.41	1.05	.29	.00	.27	.01	1.51	7.71	9.22
Dunn	1.80	1.31	.39	26.00	1.47	.37	.00	.02	.51	31.42	.45	31.87
Eau Claire	5.70	.70	.00	2.97	4.84	1.78	.00	.15	2.78	15.56	3.36	18.92
Florence	.06	.04	.00	.16	.00	.04	.00	.05	.02	.35	.02	0.37
Fond du Lac	4.65	2.16	.00	.88	2.53	1.38	.00	.36	1.65	13.21	.40	13.61
Forest	.28	.09	1.00	.15	.02	.07	.00	.09	.10	1.11	.69	1.80
Grant	2.24	3.41	.00	.35	.83	.52	255.98	.27	.78	7.77	256.61	264.38
Green	1.88	1.78	.00	5.04	1.17	.52	.00	.06	.58	10.74	.29	11.03
Green Lake	.95	.51	1.89	2.69	1.51	.66	.00	1.56	.11	9.05	.83	9.88
Iowa	1.15	1.68	.00	6.78	.23	.35	.00	.04	.44	10.30	.37	10.67
Iron	.24	.02	.00	.46	.01	.09	.00	.04	.15	.56	.45	1.01
Jackson	.70	.81	.00	4.61	.20	.35	.00	.40	.42	7.29	.20	7.49
Jefferson	4.30	1.22	3.24	10.10	7.21	.98	2.59	.18	1.06	28.00	2.88	30.88
Juneau	1.11	.50	.00	9.01	.31	.54	.00	.84	.26	11.98	.59	12.57
Kenosha	9.63	.21	.18	.73	4.21	4.36	9.05	.38	1.98	4.07	26.66	30.73
Kewaunee	.95	1.48	.90	.87	.49	.12	823.63	.08	.19	4.86	823.85	828.71
La Crosse	9.06	.69	1.59	.61	7.13	4.75	42.58	1.83	2.45	27.42	43.27	70.69
Lafayette	.77	1.92	.24	.24	.17	.13	.00	.06	.19	3.36	.36	3.72
Langlade	.91	.38	16.74	15.28	.47	.25	.00	.52	.30	20.64	14.21	34.85
Lincoln	1.45	.28	.00	.50	8.22	.29	1.45	.12	.23	2.93	9.61	12.54
Manitowoc	4.99	2.18	.00	.91	7.12	1.51	2,123.14	1.09	2.05	8.04	2,134.95	2,142.99
Marathon	6.44	3.11	.43	6.57	47.37	2.01	164.00	.84	2.26	24.23	208.80	233.03

Table 3.   Wisconsin water use by water-use purpose, water source, and county, 2005—Continued.

[Mgal/d, Million gallons per day, Thermoelectric, thermoelectric power generation]

	WITHDRAWALS, in Mgal/d											
	By water-use purpose[a]									By water source		
County	Domestic	Livestock	Aqua-culture	Irrigation	Industrial	Commercial	Thermo-electric	Mining	Public use and loss[b]	Ground water	Surface water	Total
Marinette	2.43	0.63	4.12	1.83	12.07	0.44	26.19	0.19	0.58	7.84	40.64	48.48
Marquette	.73	.37	3.97	4.77	.45	.06	.00	.00	.04	9.92	.47	10.39
Menominee	.23	.04	.72	.00	.05	.05	.00	.00	.06	.79	.36	1.15
Milwaukee	61.94	.04	.04	.43	31.11	29.88	1,075.17	.42	25.83	5.77	1,219.09	1,224.86
Monroe	2.23	1.48	.12	3.80	1.22	.75	.00	.36	.58	10.05	.49	10.54
Oconto	1.79	1.08	.65	.83	3.33	.31	.00	.34	.21	5.08	3.46	8.54
Oneida	1.64	.04	2.78	3.06	9.27	.40	15.77	.13	.60	8.10	25.59	33.69
Outagamie	8.11	1.87	.13	.63	49.96	3.02	33.01	1.16	3.11	13.57	87.43	101.00
Ozaukee	4.95	.46	.12	.64	2.18	.89	291.42	.36	1.02	9.05	292.99	302.04
Pepin	.42	.51	.00	.63	1.27	.09	.00	.00	.13	1.67	1.38	3.05
Pierce	1.51	1.08	.00	.25	.78	.43	.00	.25	.58	4.63	.25	4.88
Polk	1.61	1.01	4.87	1.18	1.32	.46	.00	.65	.46	11.03	.53	11.56
Portage	4.09	.82	.43	92.52	30.80	1.34	7.03	.58	1.61	117.01	22.21	139.22
Price	.77	.26	.00	.49	7.33	.15	3.74	.02	.28	3.13	9.91	13.04
Racine	11.89	.23	1.20	5.34	11.97	3.85	.00	1.94	6.00	14.49	27.93	42.42
Richland	.91	.92	.00	2.48	.82	.34	.00	.08	-.02	4.44	1.09	5.53
Rock	10.72	.92	.00	16.65	8.47	3.37	50.12	.84	5.22	45.75	50.56	96.31
Rusk	.58	.64	.00	.69	1.42	.09	.00	.31	.20	2.03	1.90	3.93
St. Croix	4.39	1.33	2.20	4.35	1.50	.95	.82	1.10	1.09	14.00	3.73	17.73
Sauk	3.44	1.86	.04	12.74	4.44	3.15	.00	.44	.72	26.22	.61	26.83
Sawyer	.71	.17	.72	.57	.16	.31	.00	.03	.18	2.39	.46	2.85
Shawano	1.46	1.90	.04	.23	3.82	.48	.00	.07	.53	5.23	3.30	8.53
Sheboygan	7.22	1.36	2.05	.76	10.43	1.86	377.19	.34	1.26	10.96	391.51	402.47
Taylor	.82	.90	.00	.19	.20	.08	.00	.90	.16	2.55	.70	3.25
Trempealeau	1.38	1.64	.00	5.99	1.33	.34	.00	.15	.47	10.95	.35	11.30
Vernon	1.26	1.56	1.44	.31	.19	.24	209.94	.02	.22	4.91	210.27	215.18
Vilas	.91	.01	5.50	1.17	.01	.21	.44	.04	.09	2.91	5.47	8.38
Walworth	4.10	.77	.75	2.36	2.04	2.18	.00	2.60	3.14	16.17	1.77	17.94
Washburn	.84	.23	1.21	1.71	.08	.19	.00	.01	.36	3.47	1.16	4.63
Washington	7.07	.79	.00	1.09	1.03	1.64	.00	.75	1.66	13.84	.19	14.03
Waukesha	21.59	.26	.00	1.87	3.73	8.15	.00	2.57	-.90	35.41	1.86	37.27
Waupaca	2.75	1.29	.00	8.71	5.07	.62	.00	.26	.75	17.72	1.73	19.45
Waushara	1.01	.32	.89	49.08	.54	.88	.00	.02	-.39	52.04	.31	52.35
Winnebago	11.56	.73	.00	.51	47.42	1.83	10.32	.17	4.10	10.13	66.51	76.64
Wood	3.98	1.11	.00	6.10	124.97	1.70	130.09	.23	.94	14.90	254.22	269.12
Total	316.15	72.84	81.72	401.79	585.24	118.96	6,897.93	32.52	100.91	985.91	7,622.15	8,608.06

[a]Values contain the amount of water delievered from public-supply utilities distributed by water-use purpose.

[b]A negative value occurs when the amount of water delivered is greater than the total amount of water withdrawn by the public water utilities.

Table 4.   Total water-use per capita in Wisconsin, by county, 2005.

[gal/d/person, gallons per day per person; thermoelectric, thermoelectric-power generation]

County	Including thermoelectric Total water-use per capita (gal/d/person)	Excluding thermoelectric Total water-use per capita (gal/d/person)	Total ground-water use per capita (gal/d/person)	Total surface-water use per capita (gal/d/person)
Adams	8,382.5	8,382.5	8,367.9	14.6
Ashland	5,610.4	466.9	83.4	383.5
Barron	967.0	967.0	942.3	24.7
Bayfield	3,991.4	3,991.4	1,739.3	2,252.2
Brown	2,383.2	489.0	96.6	392.5
Buffalo	98,943.0	935.7	887.9	47.8
Burnett	832.3	832.3	667.7	164.5
Calumet	245.3	245.3	178.5	66.8
Chippewa	509.1	509.1	371.5	137.5
Clark	537.5	537.5	455.1	82.4
Columbia	918.4	319.3	308.3	11.0
Crawford	401.5	401.5	359.3	42.2
Dane	779.4	187.4	180.5	6.9
Dodge	290.7	254.0	240.4	13.6
Door	662.2	662.2	470.3	191.9
Douglas	324.1	324.1	53.1	271.0
Dunn	1,655.6	1,655.6	1,632.2	23.4
Eau Claire	268.6	268.6	220.9	47.7
Florence	197.9	197.9	187.2	10.7
Fond Du Lac	212.4	212.4	206.2	6.2
Forest	491.8	491.8	303.3	188.5
Grant	8,444.0	268.3	246.9	21.4
Green	568.0	568.0	553.0	14.9
Green Lake	1,040.0	1,040.0	952.6	87.4
Iowa	802.3	802.3	774.4	27.8
Iron	262.3	262.3	145.5	116.9
Jackson	846.3	846.3	823.7	22.6
Jefferson	630.0	577.1	571.2	5.9
Juneau	1,113.4	1,113.4	1,061.1	52.3
Kenosha	286.7	202.3	38.0	164.3
Kewaunee	99,009.6	606.9	579.5	27.5
La Crosse	862.2	342.9	329.3	13.5
Lafayette	462.7	462.7	417.9	44.8
Langlade	3,804.6	3,804.6	2,253.3	1,551.3
Lincoln	898.9	795.0	210.0	585.0
Manitowoc	37,915.6	351.2	124.4	226.8
Marathon	2,760.7	817.8	281.7	536.1

Table 4. Total water-use per capita in Wisconsin, by county, 2005—Continued.

[gal/d/person, gallons per day per person; thermoelectric, thermoelectric-power generation]

County	Including thermoelectric	Excluding thermoelectric		
	Total water-use per capita (gal/d/person)	Total water-use per capita (gal/d/person)	Total ground-water use per capita (gal/d/person)	Total surface-water use per capita (gal/d/person)
Marinette	2,370.7	1,090.0	383.4	706.6
Marquette	7,068.0	7,068.0	6,748.3	319.7
Menominee	410.7	410.7	282.1	128.6
Milwaukee	1,348.0	164.7	6.4	158.4
Monroe	501.2	501.2	477.9	23.3
Oconto	856.6	856.6	509.5	347.0
Oneida	3,128.1	1,663.9	752.1	911.8
Outagamie	719.6	484.4	96.7	387.7
Ozaukee	6,198.2	217.9	185.7	32.2
Pepin	1,066.4	1,066.4	583.9	482.5
Pierce	236.7	236.7	224.5	12.1
Polk	745.3	745.3	711.2	34.2
Portage	3,571.6	3,391.2	3,001.8	389.4
Price	2,460.4	1,754.7	590.6	1,164.2
Racine	308.2	308.2	105.3	203.0
Richland	756.5	756.5	607.4	149.1
Rock	813.4	390.1	385.4	4.7
Rusk	679.9	679.9	351.2	328.7
St. Croix	469.7	448.0	370.9	77.1
Sauk	780.2	780.2	762.4	17.7
Sawyer	950.0	950.0	796.7	153.3
Shawano	450.4	450.4	276.1	174.2
Sheboygan	4,990.3	313.5	135.8	177.7
Taylor	558.4	558.4	438.1	120.3
Trempealeau	788.0	788.0	763.6	24.4
Vernon	18,204.7	443.3	402.7	40.6
Vilas	3,338.7	3,163.4	1,159.4	2,004.0
Walworth	304.1	304.1	274.1	30.0
Washburn	863.8	863.8	647.4	216.4
Washington	183.8	183.8	181.3	2.5
Waukesha	133.7	133.7	127.1	6.7
Waupaca	869.9	869.9	792.5	77.4
Waushara	8,768.8	8,768.8	8716.9	51.9
Winnebago	624.8	540.6	82.6	458.1
Wood	6,135.9	3,169.9	339.7	2,830.1
Wisconsin average	1,554.9	308.9	177.5	131.4

Water Use By Category

Total water use in Wisconsin for 2005 was determined from surface- and ground-water withdrawal estimates for eight water-use categories. These categories are presented in this report for publicly supplied water use first and then for self-supplied water use. The water-use categories ranked by total withdrawal from largest to smallest are—thermoelectric power, public supply, industrial, irrigation, non-irrigational agriculture, domestic, mining, and commercial. These withdrawals by water-use category, along with a brief description of the methods for estimating the 2005 data, are described in the following sections.

The combined total daily withdrawal for Wisconsin in 2005 was 8,608 Mgal/d of which 986 Mgal/d is from ground-water sources and 7,620 Mgal/d is from surface-water sources (tables 2 and 3). Figure 3 shows total withdrawals normalized to better illustrate water use by category and by source. Domestic, irrigation, non-irrigational agriculture, and commercial water uses are supplied mostly or exclusively from ground-water sources. Public supply and mining are about equally supplied from ground- and surface-water sources and industrial and thermoelectric-power categories are supplied primarily from surface-water sources.

Because thermoelectric-power water use is the largest water withdrawal and comes from predominantly surface-water sources, it is helpful to remove this category from certain summary information owing to the disproportionate volume. Figure 4 shows the withdrawals by water-use category excluding thermoelectric power. When thermoelectric power is excluded from the total, the distribution of ground- and surface-water withdrawals shifts from 11.5 to 57.5 percent and 88.5 to 42.5 percent, respectively (table 2), and public-supply withdrawals become the largest water-use category (table 2 and fig. 4a). Water for public supply was about equally withdrawn from both water sources (figs. 4b and 4c), 55.3 percent was from ground-water sources and 44.7 percent was from surface-water sources (table 2). The categories with the next two largest total withdrawals are industrial and irrigation, which account for about one-half (51.0 percent) of the total ground- and surface-water withdrawals (fig. 4a). Four other water-use categories make up the remaining 16.7 percent or 285 Mgal/d (fig. 4a and table 2).

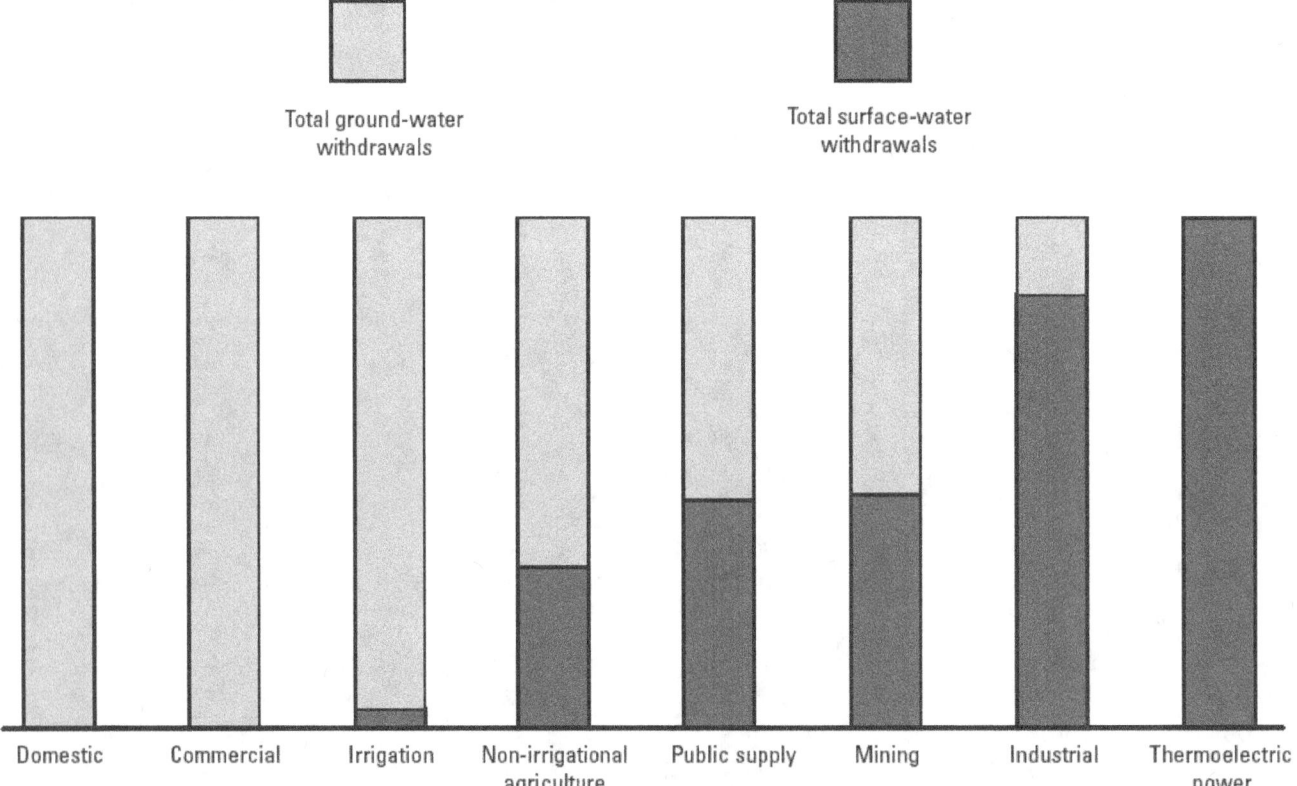

Figure 3.   Proportion of ground- and surface-water withdrawals by water-use category in Wisconsin, 2005. Non-irrigational agricultural combines water-use estimates for livestock and aquaculture. All categories except public supply describe self-supplied withdrawals.

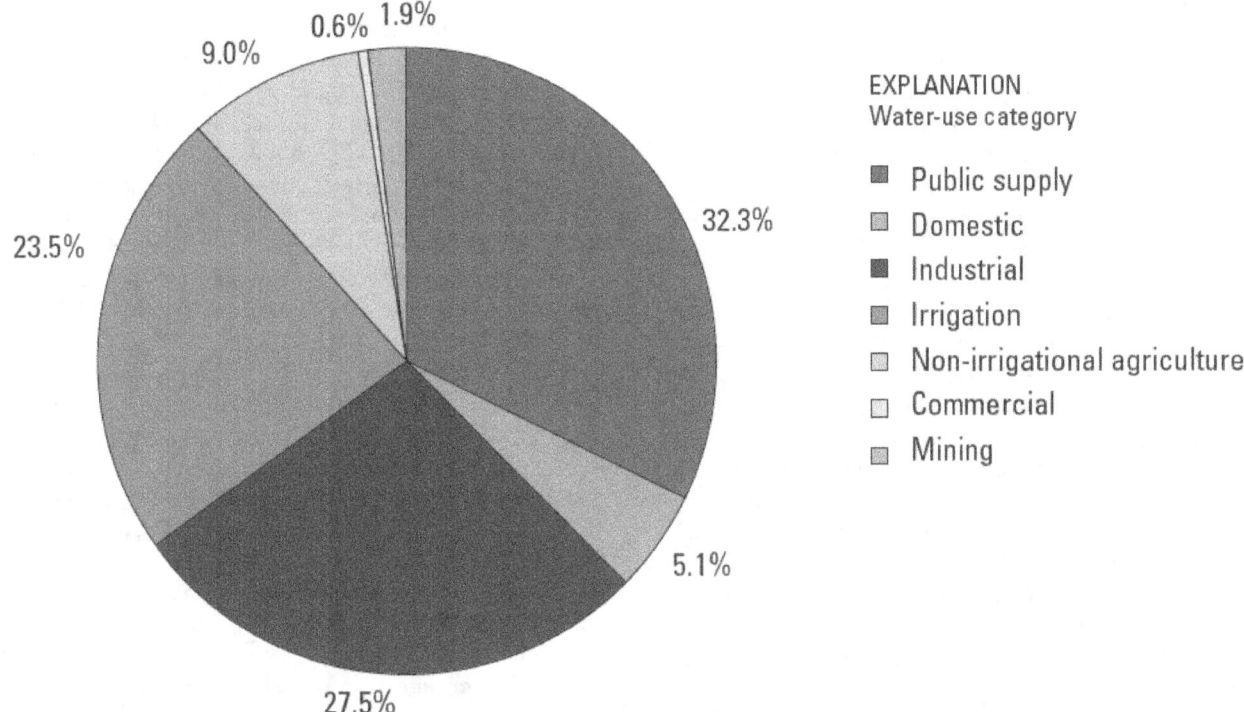

A. Total withdrawals (1,710.13 Mgal/d)

EXPLANATION
Water-use category

- Public supply
- Domestic
- Industrial
- Irrigation
- Non-irrigational agriculture
- Commercial
- Mining

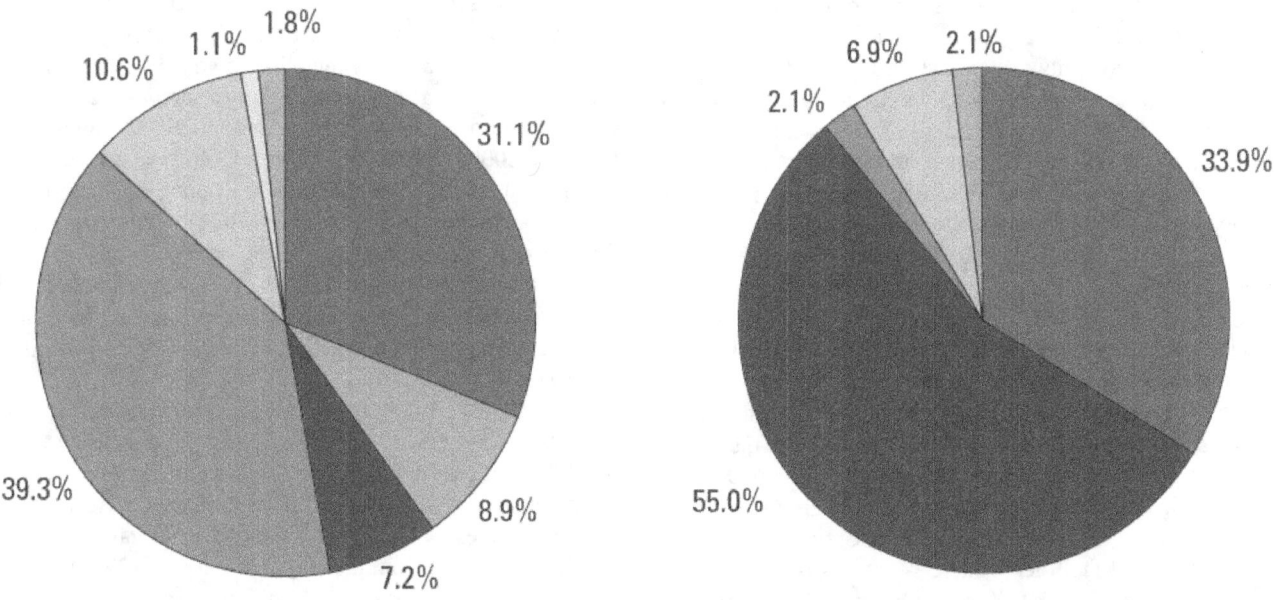

B. Ground-water withdrawals (982.54 Mgal/d)

C. Surface-water withdrawals (727.59 Mgal/d)

Figure 4.   Pie diagram showing Wisconsin water withdrawals by water-use category, excluding thermoelectric-power generation, 2005. (A) Total withdrawals. (B) Ground-water withdrawals. (C) Surface-water withdrawals. (All withdrawals correspond with values provided in table 2. Domestic and commercial water uses are assumed to have zero surface-water withdrawals. Mgal/d, million gallons per day.)

Public-Supply Water Use

The USGS defines a public water-supply system as a water-delivery system that is either publicly or privately owned and serves a year-round population of at least 25 persons or 15 service connections. Its water source may be ground water, surface water, purchased water, or any combination of those sources and delivers this water for various uses such as domestic, commercial, industrial, thermoelectric-power generation, or public use. A public supplier is often referred to as a 'water utility' or as a 'municipal-' or 'community-water supplier.' Since the first Wisconsin county-level water-use compilation for 1979, the public-supply water-use category captured predominantly municipal water-supply systems; therefore, it is recognized that not all community water-supply systems have been accounted for. This is particularly true for many Wisconsin mobile-home parks, resort communities, or private subdivision water-delivery systems that may meet the public-supply criteria but have not been identified as a community-water supplier. Populations served by these systems continue to be accounted for under the self-supplied domestic water-use category.

Much public-supply water-system infrastructure was initially constructed in the latter part of the 19th Century in response to industrial development, rapid population growth, and growing public-health concerns. Currently (2009), all cities in Wisconsin but one and most villages are identified as having a public-supply system; whereas, most towns typically do not have a public-supply system. Public suppliers served about 3.87 million people during 2005, which is approximately 70 percent of Wisconsin's total population. Wisconsin is on the low range for population on public supply in comparison with the national average of 85 percent (Hutson and others, 2004). In 2005, 1,806 of the 1,851 communities on public supply relied on ground-water sources and 45 communities relied on surface-water sources; in terms of the 611 water utilities, 587 utilities were on ground-water sources while 24 utilities were on surface-water sources. Figure 5 shows the number of utilities accounted for in each county by water source provided. The counties with the highest number of public-supply facilities are Dane with 32 facilities, Milwaukee with 23 facilities, and Grant with 21 facilities (table 5). By hydrologic unit, the Crawfish subbasin (07090002) has 44 facilities while Castle Rock (07070003) and Lower Wisconsin (07070005) subbasins have 35 and 34 facilities, respectively (table 4 and appendix 4).

When both water sources are combined, these public-supply utilities produce 552 Mgal daily and account for 32.3 percent of the 1,710 Mgal/d total amount of water withdrawn daily (excluding thermoelectric water use) (table 2 and fig. 4). They also provide about one- third (305 Mgal/d) of the total ground water withdrawn (983 Mgal/d) and one- third (247 Mgal/d) of the total surface water withdrawn (728 Mgal/d),

again excluding thermoelectric water use (table 4, fig. 4, and appendix 4). The geographic distribution and range of surface- and ground-water withdrawals for public supply by county is shown in figure 5. Counties with the largest populations withdrew the largest quantities of water. Milwaukee, Dane, Waukesha, Brown, and Racine Counties account for 48.5 percent of the total public-supply withdrawal and 49.8 percent of the total population served by public supply. The two counties with the largest surface-water withdrawals were Milwaukee and Racine Counties; the two subbasins with the largest surface-water withdrawals were Lake Michigan and Lake Winnebago subbasins. The counties with the largest ground-water withdrawals were Dane and Waukesha Counties; the subbasins with the largest ground-water withdrawals were Lower Rock River and Upper Fox River (07120006) subbasins. Five counties (Burnett, Menominee, Forest, Marquette, and Florence) and 21 subbasins (too numerous to list but identifiable in appendix 4) withdrew the least amount of water for public supply (less than 0.01 percent or 1.14 Mgal/d). These counties and subbasins are typically in far northern Wisconsin, covered by forest and (or) wetlands, have a low population density, contain an American Indian reservation, or reflect a residential population that is mostly rural agricultural.

Public-supply withdrawals are compiled for the county or subbasin in which the withdrawals occur and not by where the water is used. Populations served are compiled in the county or subbasin of residence, which is not necessarily the county or subbasin where the withdrawals occurred. This is important to note as particular counties such as Waukesha County would appear to be using less public-supply water since the 2000 compilation but in actuality are now receiving water from neighboring Milwaukee County. This also occurs for certain subbasins such as the Pike-Root where much of the Milwaukee metropolitan area is located; in this case very little public-supply withdrawal is occurring within that densely populated subbasin (appendix 1b) because the source water for that subbasin is surface water from intakes located within the Lake Michigan subbasin.

For this compilation, several steps were taken to produce the datasets used to estimate Wisconsin public-supply water use. The first step was to identify all communities served by a municipal public-supply utility or sanitary district[2]. A list of communities with water-supply systems obtained from the Public Service Commission of Wisconsin (2005) website <http://psc.wi.gov/apps/wegs/content/criteria.asp?type=water> was checked against the communities listed from WDNR and USGS data sources. Those communities with no water-supply system identified by these three sources were assumed to be self-supporting.

---

[2]A sanitary district is a municipal corporation designed for the protection of public health that is responsible for water management (provision, maintenance, and operation). This may include managing a lake or sanitary and storm sewers. A sanitary district may be urban or rural.

A. Ground water

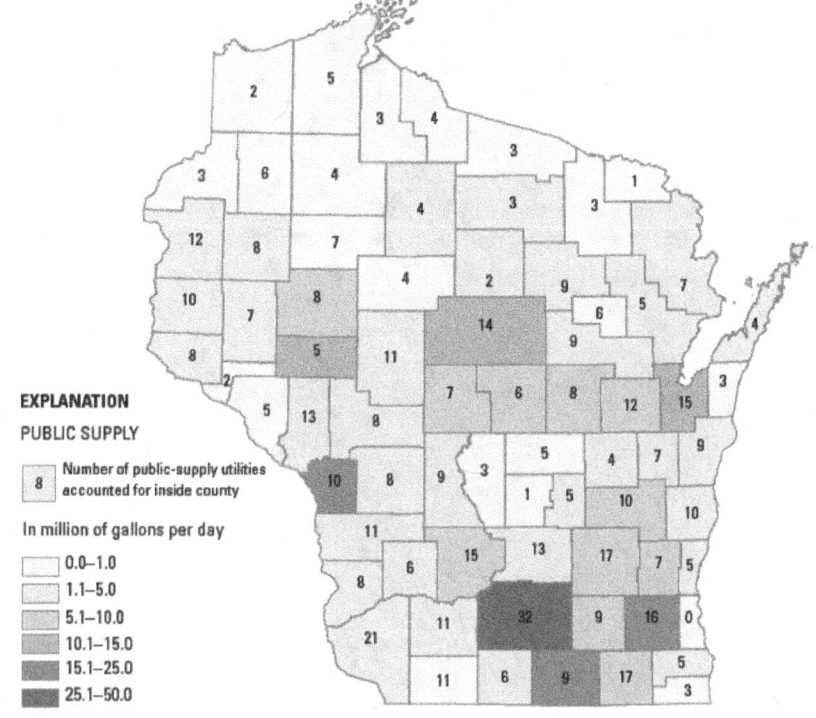

B. Surface water

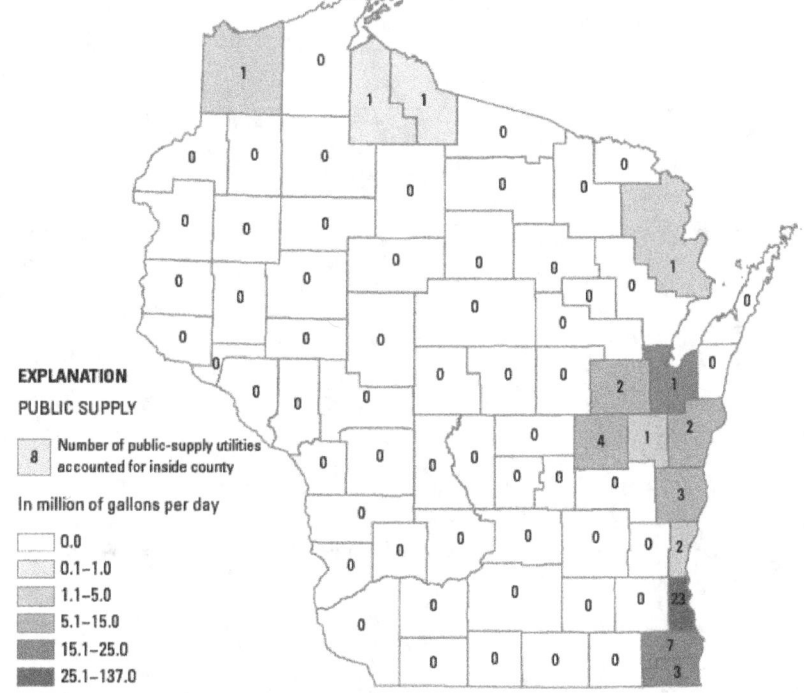

Figure 5. Public-supply water use and the number of water utilities accounted for in Wisconsin, by county, 2005. (A) Ground-water withdrawals and the number of ground-water utilities. (B) Surface-water withdrawals and the number of the surface-water utilities.

Table 5. Public-supply facilities, withdrawals, deliveries, and per-capita use in Wisconsin, by county, 2005.

[Mgal/d, million gallons per day; gal/d/person, gallons per day per person]

County	Number of public-supply facilities	Total withdrawals (Mgal/d)	Surface-water withdrawals (Mgal/d)	Ground-water withdrawals (Mgal/d)	Percent of total withdrawal		Percent of public-supply delivery to water-use category			Utility and other public use, loss, and sales to public authorities	Public-supply per capita (gal/d/person)
					Surface water	Ground water	Domestic[a]	Industrial	Commercial[b]		
Adams	3	0.54	0.00	0.54	0	100	51.5	17.2	15.7	15.7	98.4
Ashland	4	1.01	.72	.29	71.3	28.7	38.5	6.9	26.8	27.9	102.8
Barron	8	4.35	.00	4.35	0	100	22.0	38.2	11.7	28.0	214.5
Bayfield	5	.38	.00	.38	0	100	37.4	2.8	20.9	38.9	108.9
Brown	16	29.89	16.37	13.52	54.8	45.2	34.3	26.7	20.9	18.1	137.0
Buffalo	5	.53	.00	.53	0	100	47.3	8.8	13.6	30.3	97.4
Burnett	3	.32	.00	.32	0	100	43.4	3.7	28.3	24.6	103.2
Calumet	8	4.46	1.65	2.81	37	63	30.3	35.7	13.9	20.1	149.1
Chippewa	8	5.67	.00	5.67	0	100	12.6	52.4	18.9	16.1	180.5
Clark	11	1.37	.00	1.37	0	100	35.7	24.1	14.1	26.1	112.9
Columbia	13	3.39	.00	3.39	0	100	39.6	15.6	20.5	24.3	109.8
Crawford	8	1.70	.00	1.70	0	100	35.9	26.3	20.2	17.7	184.0
Dane	32	50.05	.00	50.05	0	100	50.9	3.4	27.1	18.7	130.7
Dodge	17	6.27	.00	6.27	0	100	39.3	21.4	13.8	25.5	116.8
Door	4	1.70	.00	1.70	0	100	39.1	11.0	23.6	26.4	163.2
Douglas	3	3.08	3.07	.01	99.7	0.3	90.5	0.6	8.5	.4	108.3
Dunn	7	2.27	.00	2.27	0	100	36.3	25.2	15.3	23.3	117.9
Eau Claire	5	10.26	.00	10.26	0	100	41.2	14.5	16.4	27.9	145.7
Florence	1	.08	.00	.08	0	100	42.1	.0	31.5	26.4	42.8
Fond du Lac	10	6.91	.00	6.91	0	100	43.0	14.5	18.0	24.5	107.9
Forest	3	.29	.00	.29	0	100	35.7	7.1	24.0	33.2	79.2
Grant	21	3.22	.00	3.22	0	100	43.6	16.1	15.7	24.5	102.8
Green	6	2.68	.00	2.68	0	100	38.4	21.3	18.3	22.0	138.0
Green Lake	5	1.28	.00	1.28	0	100	36.3	37.0	17.1	9.6	134.7
Iowa	11	1.32	.00	1.32	0	100	48.9	3.7	13.6	33.8	99.3
Iron	5	.39	.21	.18	53.8	46.2	36.4	2.8	22.0	38.8	101.3
Jackson	8	1.03	.00	1.03	0	100	16.5	9.7	33.8	39.9	116.4
Jefferson	9	5.84	0.00	5.84	0	100	45.5	20.9	15.3	18.3	119.1
Juneau	9	1.15	.00	1.15	0	100	40.5	1.7	34.7	23.2	101.9

Table 5. Public-supply facilities, withdrawals, deliveries, and per-capita use in Wisconsin, by county, 2005—Continued.

[Mgal/d, million gallons per day; gal/d/person, gallons per day per person]

County	Number of public-supply facilities	Total withdrawals (Mgal/d)	Surface-water withdrawals (Mgal/d)	Ground-water withdrawals (Mgal/d)	Percent of total withdrawal		Percent of public-supply delivery to water-use category				Public-supply per capita (gal/d/person)
					Surface water	Ground water	Domestic[a]	Industrial	Commercial[b]	Utility and other public use, loss, and sales to public authorities	
Kenosha	6	15.59	15.28	.31	98	2	41.4	12.8	24.5	21.4	145.5
Kewaunee	3	.84	.00	.84	0	100	45.6	18.6	13.6	22.2	100.4
La Crosse	10	15.72	.00	15.72	0	100	42.7	15.6	24.8	16.8	191.7
Lafayette	11	.84	.00	.84	0	100	45.2	19.8	12.0	23.0	104.5
Langlade	9	1.20	.00	1.20	0	100	33.4	23.7	17.7	25.3	131.0
Lincoln	2	1.31	.00	1.31	0	100	50.7	11.3	19.8	18.3	93.9
Manitowoc	11	11.68	10.02	1.66	85.8	14.2	29.6	42.5	10.7	17.3	206.7
Marathon	14	13.13	.00	13.13	0	100	32.0	36.2	14.3	17.5	155.6
Marinette	8	4.08	2.91	1.17	71.3	28.7	25.5	46.8	10.3	17.5	199.5
Marquette	1	.15	.00	.15	0	100	45.5	0.1	28.2	26.2	102.0
Menominee	6	.30	.00	.30	0	100	46.2	17.9	17.9	17.9	107.1
Milwaukee	23	137.08	137.06	.02	100	0	44.1	15.1	21.1	19.7	150.9
Monroe	8	2.63	.00	2.63	0	100	41.5	18.6	17.2	22.7	125.1
Oconto	5	1.42	.00	1.42	0	100	33.1	37.6	14.0	15.4	142.4
Oneida	3	1.88	.00	1.88	0	100	25.4	23.9	18.8	31.9	174.6
Outagamie	14	14.74	7.82	6.92	53.1	46.9	45.2	15.0	18.7	21.1	105.0
Ozaukee	7	5.79	1.20	4.59	20.7	79.3	44.8	26.7	10.1	18.4	118.8
Pepin	2	.37	.00	.37	0	100	43.4	0.0	21.4	35.2	129.4
Pierce	8	1.86	.00	1.86	0	100	44.5	2.0	22.7	30.8	90.2
Polk	12	2.41	.00	2.41	0	100	23.4	39.0	18.7	19.0	155.4
Portage	6	9.85	.00	9.85	0	100	23.9	46.6	12.7	16.8	252.7
Price	4	1.27	.00	1.27	0	100	20.9	45.8	11.0	22.2	239.6
Racine	12	26.29	22.78	3.51	86.6	13.4	31.3	32.2	14.1	22.5	191.0
Richland	6	1.15	.00	1.15	0	100	7.1	47.6	25.3	20.0	157.3
Rock	9	21.64	.00	21.64	0	100	37.3	24.7	14.0	24.0	182.8

Table 5. Public-supply facilities, withdrawals, deliveries, and per-capita use in Wisconsin, by county, 2005—Continued.

[Mgal/d, million gallons per day; gal/d/person, gallons per day per person]

County	Number of public-supply facilities	Total withdrawals (Mgal/d)	Surface-water withdrawals (Mgal/d)	Ground-water withdrawals (Mgal/d)	Percent of total withdrawal		Percent of public-supply delivery to water-use category			Utility and other public use, loss, and sales to public authorities	Public-supply per capita (gal/d/person)
					Surface water	Ground water	Domestic[a]	Industrial	Commercial[b]		
Rusk	7	0.56	0.00	0.56	0	100	38.9	8.8	16.4	35.9	96.9
Saint Croix	10	4.49	.00	4.49	0	100	47.4	7.9	19.6	25.0	118.9
Sauk	15	7.71	.00	7.71	0	100	26.6	38.0	26.1	9.3	224.2
Sawyer	4	.50	.00	.50	0	100	7.0	15.6	43.8	33.5	166.7
Shawano	9	2.42	.00	2.42	0	100	27.6	32.0	18.4	21.9	127.8
Sheboygan	13	16.38	13.44	2.94	82.1	17.9	31.0	51.1	10.2	7.7	203.1
Taylor	4	.64	.00	.64	0	100	37.7	25.1	12.0	25.3	110.0
Trempealeau	13	2.60	.00	2.60	0	100	27.2	42.4	11.9	18.5	181.3
Vernon	11	1.12	.00	1.12	0	100	45.5	14.6	20.6	19.2	94.8
Vilas	3	.33	.00	.33	0	100	30.4	.0	41.7	28.0	131.5
Walworth	17	8.00	.00	8.00	0	100	35.5	15.5	20.7	28.4	135.6
Washburn	6	.78	.00	.78	0	100	33.2	1.5	19.1	46.2	145.5
Washington	7	8.21	.00	8.21	0	100	51.7	10.1	17.2	21.0	107.6
Waukesha	16	24.40	.00	24.40	0	100	53.5	7.3	24.4	14.8	87.6
Waupaca	8	5.84	.00	5.84	0	100	20.0	58.4	8.5	13.1	261.2
Waushara	5	.69	.00	.69	0	100	17.4	22.3	37.7	22.5	115.6
Winnebago	8	17.41	14.44	2.97	82.9	17.1	51.1	15.3	10.1	23.6	141.9
Wood	7	5.66	.00	5.66	0	100	40.6	17.9	24.2	17.3	129.1
Total	611	552.39	246.97	305.42					Average		136.9

[a] The percent of domestic delivery has been corrected to include an estimate for multiple housing units that were classified as commercial by the Public Service Commission of Wisconsin.

[b] The percent of commercial delivery has been corrected to remove an estimate for domestic water use from housing units with four or more units.

The next step was to assign data for population served by each water utility to the communities in which they serve. A community boundary is not identical to the water-utility service area; therefore, the population of a community does not necessarily equal the population within the public-supply service area (Jeff Ripp, Public Service Commission of Wisconsin, oral commun., 2007; Bob Biebel, Southeastern Wisconsin Regional Planning Commission, written commun., 2007). After comparing population data from the U.S. Census Bureau for several communities against population data from the National Tap Water Quality Database (Environmental Working Group, 2005) and the Safe Drinking Water Information System (SDWIS) database (U.S. Environmental Protection Agency, 2006), it was reasonable to set population for a village or city as equivalent based on the census. Therefore, 100 percent of the 2005 adjusted census population for a village or city was applied unless actual population served was obtained from the Southeastern Wisconsin Regional Planning Commission (SEWRPC) or the WDNR and were found to be considerably dissimilar. Several communities, typically towns, were identified from SDWIS as being only partly served by a public water-supply system while the remainder of the population was self-supplied; therefore, population served and self-supplied population were adjusted accordingly.

Lastly, water-use estimates were made by summing data available from the PSC annual water-utility reports augmented with estimates based on information from SDWIS and past reported water-use data from the Wisconsin Department of Natural Resources (2005a). In general, public-supply water use is the most accurate category considering municipal public-water suppliers are regulated by the WDNR and are required to report periodic (typically monthly) water-supply withdrawals. Additionally, these suppliers must provide an annual water-utility report to the PSC that summarizes water source, withdrawal, and purchase statistics, along with other relevant information. These reports can be viewed at http://psc.wi.gov/apps/annlreport/content/munilist.aspx.

Public-Supply Deliveries, Losses, and Per-Capita Use

Reported withdrawals from each public-supply utility were allocated into four water-use delivery categories (domestic, industrial, commercial, and public authority) and one category for unsold water called 'other public use and loss.' The amount of water delivered from public-supply

systems to thermoelectric-power-generating facilities was uncertain as the deliveries are combined with industrial or other public use and loss water deliveries; however, it is expected that there are limited water utilities in which this occurs (Jeff Ripp, Public Service Commission of Wisconsin, oral commun., 2007). Deliveries for domestic and commercial use listed by the PSC were adjusted to move that portion of commercial water use sold to housing structures containing three or more units to the domestic water-use delivery category; the adjustment was based on population and housing data from the U.S. Census Bureau (2003). This adjustment can be significant for evaluating counties like Dane, Milwaukee, Brown, La Crosse, and Waukesha, which have 20 percent or more residents living in multi-unit buildings. The source and delivery of water for public supply by county in 2005 is shown in table 5; delivery data for this category were not compiled by subbasin. About 43.2 percent of delivered water is for domestic water-use purposes, while industrial and commercial water deliveries are approximately equal and sum to 50.5 percent (fig. 6b).

The amount of water for other public use and loss is calculated by subtracting the amount of water delivered from the total amount of water withdrawn by the utility. Other uses include water used by utilities (e.g., flushing and testing) and other unbilled or unmetered water uses that are unrelated to the utility (e.g., fire department uses and infrastructure damage); it does not include the amount of public-use water sold to public authorities (e.g., government buildings, public pools, or public schools). Losses consist of the unmeasurable water use resulting from leaks, water breaks, and system malfunctions. Figure 6a shows the 2005 public-supply water-withdrawal distribution. Withdrawals for other use and loss make up approximately 14.8 percent (or 81.8 Mgal/d) of the total amount of public-supply water withdrawn in 2005 (fig. 6a).

The amount of public-supply water delivered in 2005 decreased 7.9 percent since 1995 from 600 to 552 Mgal/d (delivery data were not compiled in the 2000 compilation). Meanwhile, the public-supply served population has increased 8.8 percent (about 312,000 persons) since 1995. Public-supply per capita in this compilation is calculated by dividing the total amount of public-supply water withdrawn (within the county or subbasin) by the estimated population served (within the county or subbasin). Table 5 lists public-supply per capita by county, and appendix 4 lists public-supply per capita by subbasin. Based on county data, the total public-supply per-capita use averaged 137 gal/d per person served in 2005 compared to 172 gal/d per person served in 2000.

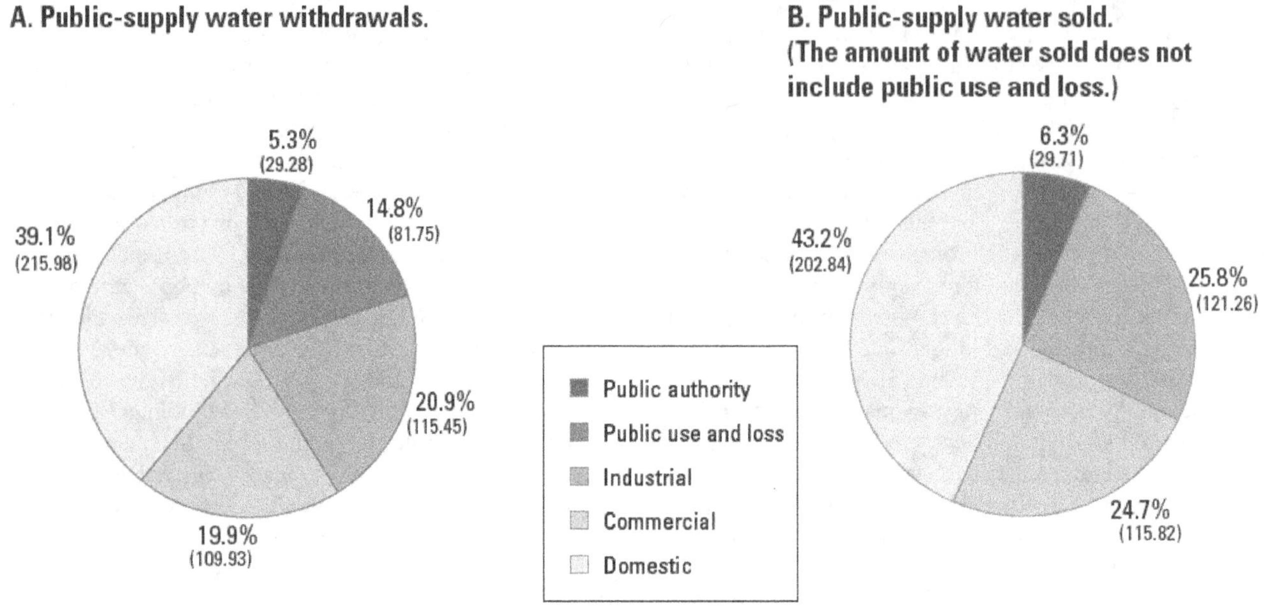

A. Public-supply water withdrawals.

5.3%
(29.28)

14.8%
(81.75)

39.1%
(215.98)

20.9%
(115.45)

19.9%
(109.93)

B. Public-supply water sold.
(The amount of water sold does not
include public use and loss.)

6.3%
(29.71)

43.2%
(202.84)

25.8%
(121.26)

24.7%
(115.82)

Legend:
- ▨ Public authority
- ▨ Public use and loss
- ▨ Industrial
- ▨ Commercial
- ☐ Domestic

Figure 6. Distribution of public-supply water use in Wisconsin, 2005. (A) Distribution of public-supply water withdrawn. (B) Distribution of public-supply water sold. (Value inside parenthesize is the amount of water in millions gallons per day.)

Self-Supplied Water Use

The USGS defines self-supplied water use as water withdrawn from a ground- or surface-water source by a user rather than being obtained from a public supply (Hutson, 2007). All self-supplied water withdrawals were estimated, because no metered data were available. Most categories for self-supplied water-use estimates were compiled more accurately at the county-level but were further estimated at the subbasin-level; the exception is for thermoelectric water use, which was accurately compiled at both levels from site-specific location information. Self-supplied categories of irrigation, commercial, industrial, livestock, and aquaculture are summarized by subbasin using an area approach, that is, the sum of the percent contribution of each county that comprises the subbasin. If the contributing percent of a county to a subbasin was <0.01 percent, the residual water-use amount was assigned to the principal subbasin of that county.

Domestic

Domestic water use includes water for household purposes, such as drinking, food preparation, bathing, washing clothes and dishes, flushing toilets, and watering lawns and gardens. Under this water-use category, self-supplied domestic water-use data are compiled and described for individual households that are self-supporting and small public-supply systems not accounted for under the public-supply category. All self-supplied domestic water withdrawals were assumed to be obtained from ground-water sources, typically a privately

owned well. It was estimated that in 2005 about 1.67 million persons were self-supporting (about 30 percent of the State's population), which is about 81,800 fewer persons than was estimated in 2000. The total self-supplied domestic water withdrawal for 2005 was estimated at 87.3 Mgal/d, which was about 9 percent less than the estimate for 2000. Self-supplied domestic population and water-use estimates during 2005 are provided, by county, in table 6. Information about publicly supplied domestic delivery during 2005 also is provided in table 6 to provide a complete evaluation of overall domestic water use in Wisconsin.

Water for self-supplied domestic use assumed that the population not served by a public-supply system used the same amount of water as the portion of the population on public supply in each county. The 2005 per-capita-use factors for self-supplied domestic use were computed from public-supply domestic delivery water-use data collected at the community level and summarized at the county level. This approach is different from previous compilations when a single per-capita-use factor was applied across the State (in 2000, the per-capita-use factor for Wisconsin was 55 gal/d per person). The 2005 per-capita-use approach for domestic water-use estimates attempted to take into account water-use differences observed in the publicly supplied domestic delivery data that often occur among exceedingly rural (or agricultural) and highly urbanized (or highly commercialized or industrialized) counties. Per-capita-use factors ranged from 19 to 83 gal/d per person and are provided by county in table 6. Five counties (Door, Douglas, Menominee, Jackson, and Sawyer) were excluded; the median domestic per-capita-use value of 49 gal/d per person, based on data from the remaining counties, was substituted. These five counties were excluded for the following reasons: seasonal tourism raised the domestic water-use delivery calculation, there was only one utility, public-supply water-use data were not available for the Indian reservation, and an error was introduced into calculation so it was decided to remove the county value from overall statistics. Overall, the county with the lowest domestic per-capita use was Florence County, with 19 gal/d per person; the county with the highest domestic per-capita use was LaCrosse County, with 83 gal/d per person. The Lower Rock River and Upper Fox River (07120006) subbasins had the largest self-supplied population (around 120,000 persons each) and withdrew around 7 Mgal/d each (appendix 2) for domestic water-use purposes. The average domestic per-capita use for Wisconsin, excluding the five counties mentioned above, was 50 gal/d per person.

Irrigation

Irrigation water use includes water applied to lands to assist in the growing of crops and pastures or to maintain vegetation on recreational lands such as parks and golf courses. This may include water applied for pre-irrigation, frost or drought protection, and chemical application. Also included for 2005 is an estimate for other irrigation that includes cemeteries, turf-grass farms, and other landscaped areas such as athletic fields, but does not include domestic lawns and gardens, which are included in the domestic water-use category. In Wisconsin, sprinkler irrigation, typically center pivot or linear move, is the primary method of irrigation; flood and micro-irrigation also are used but to a much lesser extent (U.S. Department of Agriculture–National Agricultural Statistics Service, 2004c). Only self-supplied irrigation was estimated, and the reported 2005 estimate is believed to be at the higher end of the range of possible irrigation water use. Overall irrigation water use totaled 402 Mgal/d, of which about 96 percent (387 Mgal/d) was from ground-water sources; about 4 percent (15 Mgal/d) was from surface-water sources (table 2). Most irrigation in Wisconsin (388 Mgal/d) is for agriculture (table 7).

Agricultural Irrigation

The primary crops irrigated in Wisconsin (in descending order of acreage irrigated) are assorted vegetables, corn, potatoes, soybeans, and alfalfa (U.S. Department of Agriculture–National Agricultural Statistics Service, 2004a, 2004b). The most intensively irrigated crops in Wisconsin are berries, potatoes, and corn (Bajwa and others, 1992). Irrigated crop acreage for 2005 was nearly 386,000 acres and is based on irrigated land reported by the USDA from the 2002 Agricultural Census (table 7). There were 184 more farms and about 27,000 more acres being irrigated in 2002 than were reported in the Agricultural Census of 1997. In Wisconsin, most farms use ground-water supplies to operate their irrigation systems (U.S. Department of Agriculture–National Agricultural Statistics Service, 2004c). Agricultural-irrigation water use totaled 388 Mgal/d, of which about 96 percent (374 Mgal/d) was from ground-water sources and about 4 percent (14 Mgal/d) was from surface-water sources (table 7). Surface-water sources are often used to supplement crop water requirements in times of drought. In 2005, emergency drought conditions were declared by the Governor of Wisconsin (Wisconsin Office of the Governor, 2005); if an emergency surface-water withdrawal permit was granted by the WDNR, a permitee could withdraw an amount and frequency specified in the permit for the period of the emergency, which typically was 30 days (Mary Vollbrecht, Wisconsin Department of Natural Resources, written commun., 2006). Three counties located within central Wisconsin (Portage, Waushara, and Adams) accounted for almost one-half the total agricultural irrigation (46 percent or 185 Mgal/d) and led the State in the production of vegetables (e.g., snap beans, carrots, and peas), potatoes, and corn (fig. 7a). Other counties with notable agricultural-irrigation water use (greater than 10 Mgal/d and in order of decreasing use) were Dunn, Rock, Langlade, Sauk, and Barron (table 7 and fig. 7a). The greatest number of farms that irrigate in a county does not necessarily coincide with where the largest amount of irrigation occurs.

The 2005 water-use estimation method for agricultural irrigation is dissimilar to previous compilation methods. Previous estimations were based on adjusting former water-use estimates with new totals of irrigated crop acreage and the number of wells identified for irrigation from the WDNR high-capacity well database. In 2005, a statewide water-application rate was applied as a coefficient to irrigated crop acreage reported for each county to estimate total water used for agricultural irrigation. In 2005, a water-application rate of 1,000 (gal/d)/acre (or 1.12 acre-foot/year or about 13.5 inches per year) for agricultural irrigation was adopted from a recently completed study that focused on water use in Waukesha and Sauk Counties (Gotkowitz and others, 2008). Although the irrigation water-use values reported in the study were specific to two counties and were based on limited data and information collected, using a 2005 water-application rate of 1,000 (gal/d)/acre is believed to be an improvement, considering this was a current effort reflecting primary data collected from correspondence with irrigators. Overall, the 2005 water-use estimates are believed to be at the higher end of the range of possible irrigation water use and may be unsuitable for counties where irrigation is predominantly for specialty products (e.g., sod or fruit) or in counties where there are very few farms that irrigate. The methodology for estimating irrigation water use will be refined in the 2010 compilation to better reflect the irrigation variables for each county, such as crop type, soil type, topography, and climate, and to incorporate high-capacity well data collected by the WDNR since 2007.

Table 6. Domestic water use and domestic per-capita-use in Wisconsin, by county, 2005.

[Mgal/d, million gallons per day; gal/d/person, gallons per day per person]

County	Self-supplied urban and rural population	Public-supplied urban and rural population	Percent of population on ground water	Percent of population on surface water	Public-supply domestic deliveries (Mgal/d)	Self-supplied domestic withdrawals[a] (Mgal/d)	Domestic water-use per-capita coefficient (gal/d/person)
Adams	15,338	5,490	100	0	0.28	0.78	50.8
Ashland	6,799	9,828	100	0	.39	.27	39.9
Barron	25,556	20,278	100	0	.97	1.22	47.8
Bayfield	11,655	3,490	100	0	.14	.47	40.5
Brown	20,747	218,240	56.5	43.5	10.26	1.24	48.1
Buffalo	8,531	5,437	100	0	.25	.4	46.6
Burnett	13,425	3,103	100	0	.14	.61	45.6
Calumet	14,219	29,918	97.3	2.7	1.35	.64	45.2
Chippewa	28,541	31,409	100	0	.7	.64	22.3
Clark	21,964	12,134	100	0	.49	.89	40.4
Columbia	24,480	30,884	100	0	1.66	1.31	53.6
Crawford	7,897	9,237	100	0	.61	.52	66.0
Dane	75,164	382,942	100	0	25.46	5	66.5
Dodge	34,405	53,698	100	0	2.47	1.58	46.0
Door	17,930	10,419	100	0	.67	.88	49.0
Douglas	15,764	28,444	100	0	2.79	.77	49.0
Dunn	22,456	19,252	100	0	.83	.97	43.2
Eau Claire	23,653	70,436	100	0	4.27	1.43	60.6
Florence	3,105	1,869	100	0	.03	.03	18.6
Fond Du Lac	35,271	64,066	100	0	3	1.65	46.8
Forest	6,304	3,657	100	0	.1	.18	28.0
Grant	18,357	31,314	100	0	1.41	.83	45.1
Green	15,741	19,424	100	0	1.04	.84	53.4
Green Lake	9,670	9,498	100	0	.47	.48	49.5
Iowa	10,274	13,295	100	0	.65	.5	48.8
Iron	2,799	3,850	72.9	27.1	.14	.1	37.4
Jackson	10,904	8,854	100	0	.17	.53	49.0
Jefferson	30,305	49,023	100	0	2.66	1.64	54.2
Juneau	15,433	11,292	100	0	.47	.64	41.7
Kenosha	53,372	107,172	26.5	73.5	7.17	2.46	59.2
Kewaunee	12,471	8,369	100	0	.38	.57	45.8
La Crosse	26,969	81,989	100	0	6.82	2.24	83.2
Lafayette	8,270	8,040	100	0	.38	.39	47.1
Langlade	11,574	9,161	100	0	.4	.51	44.1
Lincoln	16,367	13,952	100	0	.67	.78	47.8
Manitowoc	25,428	56,521	43.1	56.9	3.44	1.55	60.9
Marathon	44,528	84,413	100	0	4.22	2.22	50.0
Marinette	22,958	20,448	72.9	27.1	1.17	1.26	50.9

Table 6.   Domestic water use and domestic per-capita-use in Wisconsin, by county, 2005—Continued.

[Mgal/d, million gallons per day; gal/d/person, gallons per day per person]

County	Self-supplied urban and rural population	Public-supplied urban and rural population	Percent of population on ground water	Percent of population on surface water	Public-supply domestic deliveries (Mgal/d)	Self-supplied domestic withdrawals[a] (Mgal/d)	Domestic water-use per-capita coefficient (gal/d/person)
Marquette	13,764	1,473	100	0	0.07	0.66	47.7
Menominee	1,781	2,799	100	0	.14	.09	49.0
Milwaukee	13,000	908,654	1.1	98.9	61.07	.87	67.2
Monroe	21,611	21,033	100	0	1.1	1.13	52.1
Oconto	27,700	9,966	100	0	.47	1.32	47.5
Oneida	26,227	10,767	100	0	.48	1.16	48.3
Outagamie	30,658	140,348	53.2	46.8	6.66	1.45	51.3
Ozaukee	37,344	48,728	87.3	12.7	2.62	2.33	62.3
Pepin	4,515	2,865	100	0	.16	.26	56.7
Pierce	18,477	20,625	100	0	.8	.71	38.7
Polk	28,815	15,514	100	0	.56	1.05	36.4
Portage	28,604	38,981	100	0	2.36	1.73	60.7
Price	9,915	5,305	100	0	.27	.5	50.3
Racine	58,089	137,619	53.5	46.5	8.36	3.53	60.7
Richland	11,090	7,313	100	0	.36	.55	49.3
Rock	39,128	118,410	100	0	8.06	2.66	68.1
Rusk	9,416	5,782	100	0	.22	.36	37.8
St. Croix	39,391	37,753	100	0	2.15	2.24	56.9
Sauk	23,355	34,391	100	0	2.05	1.39	59.7
Sawyer	13,970	3,005	100	0	.03	.68	49.0
Shawano	22,391	18,944	100	0	.67	.79	35.3
Sheboygan	33,960	80,650	47.8	52.2	5.08	2.14	62.9
Taylor	13,949	5,817	100	0	.24	.58	41.6
Trempealeau	13,477	14,335	100	0	.71	.67	49.6
Vernon	17,236	11,819	100	0	.51	.75	43.3
Vilas	19,820	2,510	100	0	.1	.81	41.0
Walworth	40,858	58,986	100	0	1.97	2.13	48.1
Washburn	11,241	5,360	100	0	.26	.58	48.0
Washington	49,835	76,323	100	0	4.28	2.79	56.1
Waukesha	100,282	278,689	100	0	15.88	5.71	57.0
Waupaca	30,200	22,363	100	0	1.17	1.58	52.3
Waushara	18,821	5,968	100	0	.24	.77	40.7
Winnebago	36,816	122,666	33.9	66.1	8.89	2.67	72.5
Wood	31,379	43,855	100	0	2.32	1.66	52.8
Total	1,665,739	3,870,462			228.83	87.32	
						Average	49.6
						Median	49.0

[a]It is possible that domestic withdrawal will not recalculate precisely to the value listed in this table as some community populations within a county have been updated without modifying the applied domestic per-capita-use coefficient.

Table 7.   Irrigation water use in Wisconsin, by county, 2005.

[Mgal/d, million gallons per day; --, since no water-use sites were identified, no estimate was provided; the surface-water column for other irrigation was removed since no water-use sites of this source type were identified]

County	Total irrigation			Crop irrigation				Golf course irrigation			Other irrigation	
	Total withdrawal (Mgal/d)	Total ground-water withdrawal (Mgal/d)	Total surface-water withdrawal (Mgal/d)	Ground water (Mgal/d)	Surface water (Mgal/d)	Number of farms that irrigate	Irrigated acreage (acres)	Ground water (Mgal/d)	Surface water (Mgal/d)	Number of golf courses that irrigate	Ground water (Mgal/d)	Number of sites identified with other irrigation
Adams	44.16	44.09	0.06	44.00	0.06	64	44,060	0.08	0.00	4	0.01	3
Ashland	.08	.03	.04	.00	.04	4	14	.03	.01	4	--	--
Barron	10.36	10.06	.30	9.94	.29	33	10,232	.11	.01	9	.01	3
Bayfield	.17	.16	.01	.10	--	19	97	.06	.01	6	--	--
Brown	.90	.60	.31	.10	.29	30	391	.37	.02	19	.12	10
Buffalo	2.34	2.22	.12	2.16	.12	18	2,278	.04	.00	2	.02	3
Burnett	.40	.38	.02	.15	.02	6	169	.08	.00	5	.15	3
Calumet	.35	.13	.22	.00	.19	8	44	.09	.03	6	.04	3
Chippewa	3.28	2.95	.34	2.79	.33	45	3,116	.10	.01	7	.07	7
Clark	.53	.07	.47	.05	.46	45	317	.01	.00	2	--	--
Columbia	1.72	1.65	.07	1.50	.07	46	1,562	.14	.01	9	.01	1
Crawford	.31	.02	.29	.00	.29	22	135	.02	.00	2	--	--
Dane	6.16	6.00	.16	5.15	.12	97	5,273	.68	.04	30	.17	20
Dodge	.64	.60	.04	.48	.02	28	496	.11	.02	6	.01	1
Door	1.10	1.07	.03	.81	.02	41	832	.19	.01	12	.07	4
Douglas	.41	.40	.01	.30	--	16	303	.10	.01	8	--	--
Dunn	26.00	25.69	.31	25.58	.31	61	25,890	.06	.00	4	.05	3
Eau Claire	2.97	2.87	.10	2.63	.10	25	2,730	.13	.01	7	.11	6
Florence	.16	.16	.00	.15	--	3	154	.01	.00	1	--	--
Fond du Lac	.88	.87	.01	.78	.01	24	781	.10	.00	6	--	--
Forest	.15	.01	.14	.00	.14	3	127	.01	.00	1	--	--
Grant	.35	.15	.20	.09	.20	23	291	.05	.00	5	--	--
Green	5.04	4.96	.09	4.64	.08	42	4,723	.07	.00	5	.24	4
Green Lake	2.69	2.65	.04	2.51	.03	19	2,546	.11	.01	4	.03	4
Iowa	6.78	6.60	.18	6.44	.18	42	6,618	.11	.00	4	.05	5
Iron	0.46	0.24	0.22	0.21	0.21	5	423	0.03	0.01	3	--	--

Table 7. Irrigation water use in Wisconsin, by county, 2005—Continued.

[Mgal/d, million gallons per day; --, since no water-use sites were identified, no estimate was provided; the surface-water column for other irrigation was removed since no water-use sites of this source type were identified]

County	Total irrigation			Crop irrigation				Golf course irrigation			Other irrigation	
	Total withdrawal (Mgal/d)	Total ground-water withdrawal (Mgal/d)	Total surface-water withdrawal (Mgal/d)	Ground water (Mgal/d)	Surface water (Mgal/d)	Number of farms that irrigate	Irrigated acreage (acres)	Ground water (Mgal/d)	Surface water (Mgal/d)	Number of golf courses that irrigate	Ground water (Mgal/d)	Number of sites identified with other irrigation
Jackson	4.60	4.49	.12	4.43	.12	54	4,547	.02	.00	2	0.04	5
Jefferson	10.10	10.02	.08	9.59	.08	39	9,668	.09	.00	5	.33	23
Juneau	9.01	8.87	.14	8.81	.14	29	8,945	.04	.00	2	.02	2
Kenosha	.73	.55	.19	.32	.17	28	489	.13	.01	9	.10	9
Kewaunee	.87	.83	.04	.78	.04	12	818	.05	.00	3	--	--
La Crosse	.61	.48	.13	.11	.10	11	207	.17	.03	11	.21	20
Lafayette	.23	.10	.14	.07	.14	9	207	.03	.00	2	--	--
Langlade	15.27	14.74	.54	14.71	.54	50	15,244	.03	.00	3	--	--
Lincoln	.50	.40	.10	.33	.10	34	428	.05	.00	4	.02	2
Manitowoc	.91	.44	.47	.32	.46	23	441	.11	.02	9	.01	1
Marathon	6.57	3.48	3.09	3.37	3.06	76	6,431	.11	.02	8	.01	1
Marinette	1.83	1.66	.17	1.49	.14	21	1,626	.15	.03	11	.02	2
Marquette	4.77	4.70	.07	4.64	.07	38	4,709	.04	.00	2	.02	3
Menominee	.00	.00	.00	--	--	--	--	--	--	--	--	--
Milwaukee	.43	.39	.04	.03	.02	25	53	.36	.02	22	.00	1
Monroe	3.81	3.63	.17	3.53	.17	87	3,700	.05	.00	4	.05	4
Oconto	.83	.78	.05	.64	.04	18	676	.13	.01	9	.02	1
Oneida	3.06	2.85	.21	2.73	.12	24	2,845	.12	.09	8	.00	1
Outagamie	.63	.41	.22	.11	.21	21	167	.24	.01	12	.06	5
Ozaukee	.64	.49	.15	.22	.04	26	263	.24	.11	11	.03	4
Pepin	.62	.55	.08	.53	.08	8	609	.01	.00	1	--	--
Pierce	.25	.23	.02	.06	.02	29	84	.17	.00	5	--	--
Polk	1.18	1.10	.08	.96	.08	28	1,038	.10	.01	7	.04	2
Portage	92.52	92.16	.36	91.97	.36	180	92,330	.09	.01	5	.10	10
Price	.48	.46	.03	.44	0.02	6	467	0.01	0.00	2	--	--
Racine	5.34	5.03	.31	4.70	.29	41	4,986	.14	.02	10	0.19	12

Table 7. Irrigation water use in Wisconsin, by county, 2005—Continued.

[Mgal/d, million gallons per day; --, since no water-use sites were identified, no estimate was provided; the surface-water column for other irrigation was removed since no water-use sites of this source type were identified]

County	Total irrigation			Crop irrigation				Golf course irrigation			Other irrigation	
	Total withdrawal (Mgal/d)	Total ground-water withdrawal (Mgal/d)	Total surface-water withdrawal (Mgal/d)	Ground water (Mgal/d)	Surface water (Mgal/d)	Number of farms that irrigate	Irrigated acreage (acres)	Ground water (Mgal/d)	Surface water (Mgal/d)	Number of golf courses that irrigate	Ground water (Mgal/d)	Number of sites identified with other irrigation
Richland	2.48	1.52	.96	1.47	.96	21	2,432	.02	.00	2	.03	1
Rock	16.64	16.58	.07	16.25	.05	70	16,297	.21	.02	17	.12	14
Rusk	.70	.37	.33	.36	.28	10	94	.01	.04	2	--	--
St Croix	4.37	4.31	.06	3.92	.06	46	3,974	.25	.01	13	.12	11
Sauk	12.84	12.67	.17	12.33	.14	73	12,470	.22	.03	10	.02	2
Sawyer	.56	.49	.07	.35	.06	12	407	.12	.01	10	.03	3
Shawano	.26	.13	.14	.04	.12	17	153	.06	.02	4	--	--
Sheboygan	.76	.57	.19	.11	.17	19	32	.33	.01	13	.14	9
Taylor	.19	.01	.18	.00	.17	6	17	.01	.00	2	--	--
Trempealeau	5.99	5.87	.12	5.70	.12	26	5,815	.06	.00	6	.11	4
Vernon	.32	.04	.27	.00	.27	38	75	.03	.00	2	.01	1
Vilas	1.17	1.16	.01	1.04	--	13	1,037	.13	.01	9	--	--
Walworth	2.36	1.91	.45	1.44	.41	48	1,848	.37	.04	17	.11	10
Washburn	1.71	1.71	.00	1.58	--	26	1,577	.09	.00	4	.04	2
Washington	1.09	.98	.11	.67	.09	34	761	.28	.01	11	.04	4
Waukesha	1.86	1.58	.29	.52	.25	48	769	.73	.03	35	.33	17
Waupaca	8.71	8.23	.48	8.03	.45	47	8,478	.14	.03	12	.05	5
Waushara	49.08	48.81	.27	48.65	.27	94	48,917	.09	.00	2	.08	11
Winnebago	.52	.35	.16	.07	.14	21	205	.23	.03	13	.06	5
Wood	6.10	5.96	.14	5.80	.14	102	5,932	.07	.01	6	.09	9
Total	401.92	386.72	15.21	373.78	14.27	2457	385,870	9.01	.94	528	3.79	296

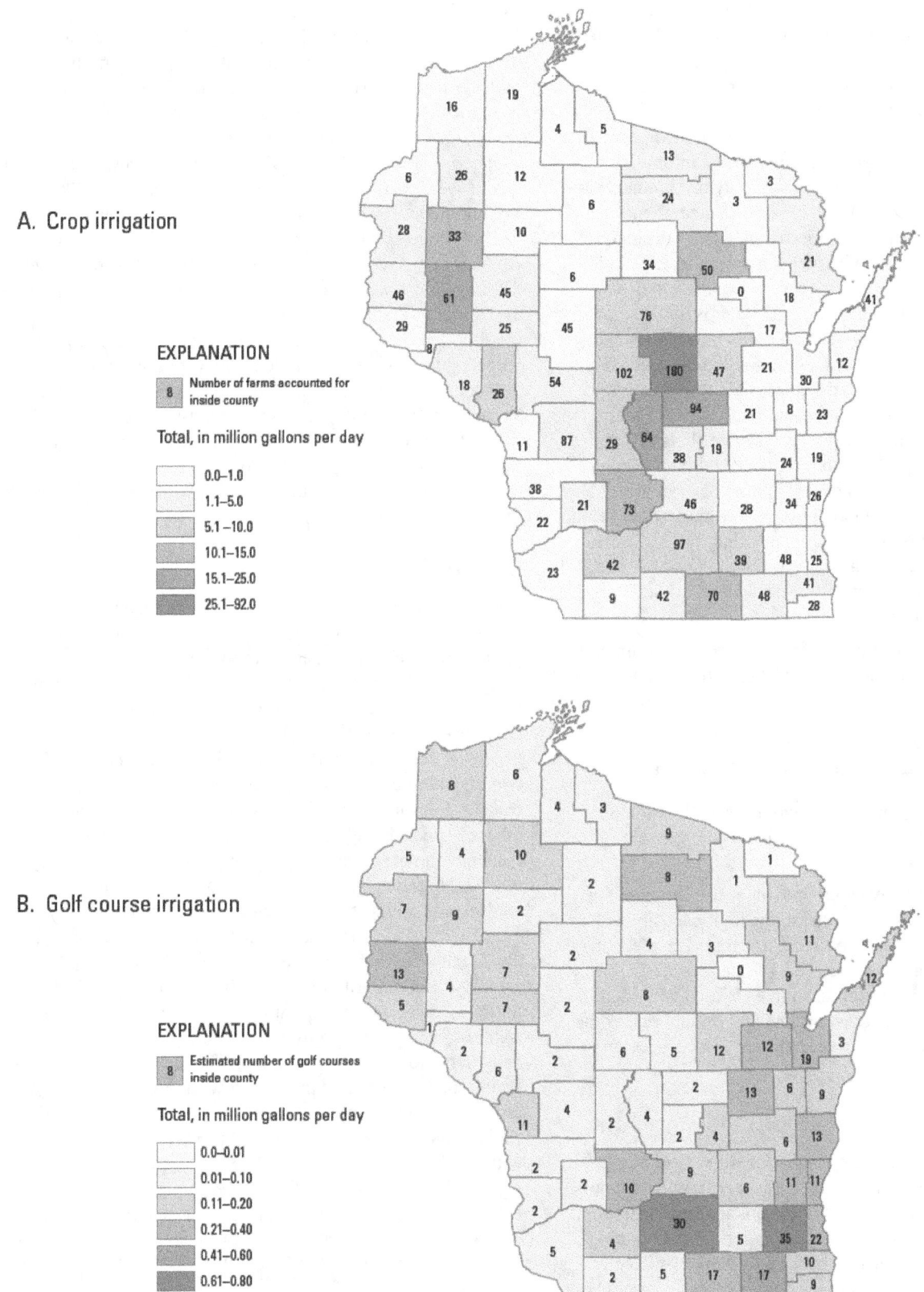

Figure 7. Irrigation water use and the approximate number of facilities that irrigate in Wisconsin, by county, 2005. (A) Total crop irrigation and the number of farms accounted for, by county, that irrigate (U.S. Department of Agriculture–National Agricultural Statistics Service, 2004b). (B) Total golf course irrigation and the estimated number of golf courses, by county, that irrigate.

The surface-water use estimate for agricultural irrigation was based on data retrieved from the WDNR surface-water withdrawal-permit database in 2006 (Mary Vollbrecht, Wisconsin Department of Natural Resources, unpub. data, 2006). The applicant's name was used to assign the most likely use for the withdrawal; therefore, withdrawal records identified for other uses such as remediation, mining, or aquaculture were removed. If a record only had an individual's name, it was assumed to be for agricultural irrigation. Ultimately 810 records were selected, and key information such as frequency of the withdrawal, pump rate, expected pump time, and irrigated acreage were extracted, when available, for analysis. There were 23 records that contained all data fields previously listed. From this information the combined duration for a surface-water withdrawal, on average, was 22 days, with a median duration value for 14 days and an average surface-water application rate of 766.9 (gal/d)/acre or a median value of 591.3 (gal/d)/acre. There were 294 records with reported pump-rate data, with an average value of 384 gal/min or a median value of 350 gal/min. There were 260 records with reported irrigated acreage; the average value was 49.9 acres, and the median value was 38.5 acres. If the amount of the withdrawal was reported, it was used; otherwise, surface-water withdrawals for agricultural irrigation were estimated as follows:

1. If acreage is known but pump rate is not, the estimate is based on a ground-water application rate of 1,000 (gal/d)/acre for 14 days; or

2. If pump rate is known but acreage is not, the estimate is based on reported pump rate for a 14-day duration; or

3. If pump rate and acreage are not known, the estimate is based on median pump capacity of 350 gal/min for a 14-day duration.

For a county to have a ground-water-use estimate for irrigation, it must have had at least one high-capacity well for irrigation approved by the WDNR; otherwise, the water source for the county was assumed 100 percent surface water. If the county had, at a minimum, one irrigation well identified, the ground-water estimate was calculated by subtracting the surface-water estimate from the total water for agricultural-irrigation estimate.

Golf Course Irrigation

Many factors affect the amount of water used at golf courses including course design, acreage, irrigation systems, soils, availability of water for irrigation, and local irrigation practices. Typically, more water is applied for maintaining greens and tees than what is required for fairways (Kenny, 2004; Pira, 1997). Information about golf courses throughout Wisconsin were pulled together from three websites into a master list and then correlated with available water-use and

well-construction data (GolfLink, 2009; GolfWisconsin, 2009; U.S. Golf Course Finder, 2008). All sites were assumed to have some irrigation requirement including pond-filling of water hazards. About one-half of the listed golf courses were identified as having irrigation wells; for those courses, the source of irrigation water was assumed to be 100 percent supplied by ground-water sources. The withdrawal was based on the average of reported water-use rates prior to 1990 or an irrigation coefficient based on the number of holes (table 7). For golf courses with no wells identified, it is uncertain whether they have an irrigation requirement and if so, whether the irrigation water was publicly or self-supplied. Therefore, the estimated water use in table 7 was reduced by one-half and the source water was allocated 85 percent ground water and 15 percent surface water. In 2005, irrigation water use for 528 golf courses was estimated to total 10 Mgal/d, of which about 91 percent (9 Mgal/d) was from ground-water sources and about 9 percent (1 Mgal/d) was from surface-water sources (table 8). Waukesha and Dane Counties led the State in the overall number of golf courses and golf course irrigation water use (fig. 7b).

Other Irrigation

Other irrigation includes water use at such places as athletic fields, cemeteries, tree nurseries, and commercial gardens (e.g., botanical gardens and garden centers). Irrigation estimates under this category were unaccounted for in previous compilations and are now part of the overall 2005 irrigation water-use estimate. Table 9 lists all other irrigation water-use purposes[3] considered for 2005 and the corresponding default withdrawal rates. This water-use category was added for three reasons: (1) various data and information were available for other uses besides agricultural or golf course irrigation; (2) to complete the irrigation water-use estimate; and (3) to evaluate whether there are other irrigation trends, especially with landscaping and turf grass, occurring in Wisconsin.

Table 7 shows the distribution of the 296 sites in 51 of the 72 counties that were identified with the other-irrigation category. The majority of these irrigation sites were identified for landscaping water use (table 9). The estimated ground-water use was 3.79 Mgal/d, which is 1 percent of the total daily irrigation water use estimated for 2005. Jefferson and Waukesha Counties had the largest withdrawals: 0.33 Mgal/d each. Jefferson County had the most irrigation sites identified (23) in this category, followed by LaCrosse and Dane Counties with 20 sites each.

---

[3] Some overlap may occur for orchards and sod-growing facilities as these locations produce specialty agricultural products and were mostly included in irrigated acreage reported by the Agricultural Census; however, identified wells and their associated water-use estimates were considered other irrigation rather than agricultural irrigation for principal crops in the 2005 compilation. The combined withdrawals identified for these sites are minimal, and a correction was not applied to adjust the agricultural-irrigation water-use estimate.

Table 8. Golf course irrigation water-use coefficients applied in Wisconsin, 2005.

[Mgal/yr, million gallons per year]

Number of holes	Estimated water use (Mgal/yr)[1]	Average irrigated acreage
9	5	15
18	10	30
27	15	45
36	20	60
45	25	75

[1]Data provided by Tom Schwab, O.J. Noer Turf Grass Research & Education Facility, oral commun., 2001

Table 9. Number of irrigation wells identified and the default withdrawal applied for other irrigation water-use purposes, in Wisconsin, 2005.

[Mgal/yr, million gallons per year; MNDNR WAPP, Minnesota Department of Natural Resources Water Appropriations Permit Program]

Other irrigation water-use purpose	Number of wells identified with other irrigation	Default ground-water withdrawal (Mgal/yr)	Water-use estimation method
Cemetery	4	6.59	applied water-use data from MNDNR WAPP
Sod[a]	27	6.46	applied water-use data from MNDNR WAPP
Athletic field	28	3.98	applied water-use data from MNDNR WAPP
Landscaping	118	3.98	applied water-use data from MNDNR WAPP
Nursery	45	2.65	applied water-use data from MNDNR WAPP
Greenhouse	17	2.65	assumed similar to nursery water-use purpose
Flower grower	6	2.65	assumed similar to nursery water-use purpose
Evergreen farm	9	2.65	assumed similar to nursery water-use purpose
Seed farms	8	2.65	assumed similar to nursery water-use purpose
Orchard[a]	1	2.33	applied water-use data from MNDNR WAPP
Unspecified other	25	variable	calculation based upon 5 days per month for 4 growing season months at the reported normal pumpage rate
Specialty commodities[b]	8	variable	calculation based upon 5 days per month for 4 growing season months at the reported normal pumpage rate

[a]Some water-use estimates for other irrigation at orchards and sod farms may be duplicated if the identified sites were already included in irrigated acreage reported by the 2002 Census of Agriculture and then estimated under crop irrigation.

[b]Specialty commodities include evergreens, sod[a], flower or seed growing, and other specialty edibles such as mint, ginseng, and mushrooms that are not considered principal crops.

Water use estimated in this category was all ground water as no surface-water withdrawals for other irrigation were identified. Ground-water sites, identified as active, were extracted from the WDNR high-capacity well database website and from the WDNR Water Well Data CD-ROM (Wisconsin Department of Natural Resources, 2005b, 2007). The ground-water-use estimates were determined either by the average of reported water-use data prior to 1990 or by a water-purpose-based default estimate for each well and then summarized by county. The water-use default values were derived from a concurrent investigation focusing on the Lake Michigan Basin where data from the adjacent State of Minnesota's Department of Natural Resources Water Appropriations Permit Program (MNDNR WAPP) were analyzed for wells of similar water-use purpose. When the water purpose of a well did not meet one of the category methods listed in table 9, a water-use estimate was based upon the reported normal well-pumpage rate assuming the well was active at least 5 days per month during the 4-month summer growing season. This approach resulted in well-specific estimates that reflected the pump-capacity magnitude and ranged from 0.01 Mgal/d (for a garden center) to 22.2 Mgal/d (for a flooded area).

Non-Irrigational Agriculture

Non-irrigational agriculture includes two subcategories of water use: livestock and aquaculture. Livestock refers to the farming of animals that are associated with the production of meat, milk, poultry, eggs, and fur, whereas, aquaculture refers to the farming of animals that live in water within a controlled environment (Kenny, 2004). Each subcategory is provided separately to allow comparison with former USGS Wisconsin water-use compilations in which aquaculture was not estimated. Each subcategory withdraws approximately the same amount of water overall (table 2).

Livestock

Livestock water use includes water used for stock watering, feed lots, dairy farming, and other farm needs such as for cooling or sanitation (e.g., animal-cooling sprinkler systems, milk parlor, or equipment washing). Wisconsin's Agricultural Census data for livestock since 1959 were reviewed confirming that the number of livestock facilities has been steadily declining, which reflects the shift from numerous small family farms to fewer large livestock facilities (Hanson, 2002). The Agricultural Censuses also show that while livestock-animal counts vary the overall counts appear to be declining for most livestock types with the exception of poultry (U.S. Department of Agriculture–National Agricultural Statistics Service, 1994, 1999, 2004b). In prior compilations, other specialty animals (mink, llamas/alpaca, bison, rabbits, deer, elk, and ostrich/emu) were not included, but these livestock types are now part of the overall estimate. Livestock water use is rarely monitored or measured by the farmer (Kenny, 2004) and is therefore estimated by livestock counts and livestock-specific water-use coefficient estimates.

Total livestock water use in Wisconsin for 2005 was estimated at 72.8 Mgal/d. As with previous water-use compilations, the water-use coefficients listed in table 10 combine surface- and ground-water sources. The WI WSC will continue to use the proportion of 90 percent from ground-water sources and 10 percent from surface-water sources (streams, creeks, and ponds). Therefore, in 2005, 65.6 Mgal/d was estimated to be from ground-water sources and 7.27 Mgal/d was estimated to be from surface-water sources (table 2). In 2005, dairy cows made up 59 percent of the total livestock water use while beef and other cattle made up the next largest use with 35 percent. County estimates for livestock water use are provided in table 11. Grant, Marathon, and Clark Counties in southwest and central Wisconsin have the most cattle by count, and each use more than 3 Mgal/d of water for these livestock. Subbasin estimates for livestock water use are provided in appendix 2. Manitowoc-Sheboygan Rivers subbasin in eastern Wisconsin along Lake Michigan (fig. 2) used 5.73 Mgal/d and was the subbasin with the largest livestock water use, followed by Lower Wisconsin River (4.47 Mgal/d) and Upper Rock River (4.22 Mgal/d). The total livestock water-use estimate is 9.8 percent (6.51 Mgal/d) greater than the 2000 estimate.

The amount of water per animal combines daily water consumption with other non-consumptive livestock-related water use for everyday operations on the farm, such as for cooling or sanitation. By and large, dairy cows have the greatest water-use requirement (table 10); which depends on, for example, milk yield, air temperature, quality of available water, and moisture and salt content in the diet (Linn, 1997). Lactating dairy cows generally require 2 to 4 pounds of water (approximately ¼ to ½ gal) per pound of milk produced (Linn, 1997). Updated livestock water-use coefficients (table 11) were provided by the Wisconsin Department of Agriculture, Trade and Consumer Protection (DATCP) with units in gallons per day per animal (John Marks, Wisconsin Department of Agriculture, Trade and Consumer Protection, written commun., 2006). Most coefficients have been slightly modified since previous compilations. Total livestock water use in each county was based on a livestock-specific head count and water-use coefficient for all livestock types considered.

Aquaculture

Aquaculture water use includes farming of animals that live in water, such as fish and shellfish, within a confined space and under controlled feeding, sanitation, and harvesting procedures (Kenny, 2004). Aquaculture for Wisconsin is an optional water-use category, and water use prior to 1990 was not estimated; however, because it is a growing economic activity of Wisconsin (Wisconsin Department of Agriculture, Trade and Consumer Protection, 1998), a more in-depth evaluation was initiated with the 2000 compilation.

Table 10.   Livestock water-use coefficients by animal type applied in Wisconsin, 2005.

[gal/d/animal, gallons per day per animal]

Livestock type	Water-use coefficient[1], in gal/d/animal
Dairy cows	35
Beef and other cattle	12
Swine	3.5
Chickens; non-specific	.06
Chickens; egg-layers	.09
Turkey	.12
Sheep/lambs	2
Goats	2
Horses/mules	10
Llamas/alpaca	2
Ostrich/emu	2
Captive deer/elk/bison	1
Mink/rabbits	.05

[1] Values provided by John Marks, Wisconsin Department of Agriculture, Trade and Consumer Protection, 2006

According to the 2005 Census of Aquaculture, there were 84 fish farms in Wisconsin for 2005, which was down slightly from the 95 fish farms reported in 1998 (U.S. Department of Agriculture–National Agricultural Statistics Service, 2006). In this compilation, 83 aquacultural facilities were accounted for. In 2005, it was estimated that of the 81.7 Mgal/d withdrawn for aquaculture, a total of 47.1 percent (38.5 Mgal/d) was withdrawn from ground-water sources and 52.9 percent (43.2 Mgal/d) was withdrawn from surface-water sources (table 2). These estimates are similar to the proportions of source water reported in the 2005 Census of Aquaculture, although it is possible that the reported on-farm surface water may have included flow from artesian wells (U.S. Department of Agriculture–National Agricultural Statistics Service, 2004c), whereas these wells are considered ground water in this compilation. These estimates exclude in-stream water use, although this is not atypical for an aquacultural facility if, for example, the operation uses surface water within a waterway or water body to transport fish between locations or to provide habitat for aquatic life but does not divert water. A few facilities withdraw from both ground- and surface-water sources. In 2005, it was estimated that about 72 percent of the facilities withdrew ground water to some extent. The 2005 total aquacultural water-use estimate was 16.4 percent (11.5 Mgal/d) more than the 2000 estimate with an estimated 42.2 percent (12.8 Mgal/d) increase in surface water and 3.3 percent (1.32 Mgal/d) decrease in ground water.

Table 12 summarizes aquacultural water use and the number of facilities by county, and appendix 2 summarizes aquacultural water use by subbasin. Langlade County had the most aquacultural facilities (seven were identified).

Two counties and two subbasins had aquacultural water use greater than 10 Mgal/d, which was largely surface-water use in Langlade and Bayfield Counties and Wolf and Lake Superior subbasins. Polk County (4.83 Mgal/d) and the Upper Fox River subbasin (07120006) (5.50 Mgal/d) used the most ground water for aquaculture.

Data about production, water source, and water use were collected in 2000 from inquiries sent to Federal and State aquacultural facilities; additional private facilities were contacted in 2007. Most facilities had some key information available on their websites. For facilities that did not respond to an inquiry but were identified as having high-capacity ground-water wells, the average of reported withdrawals prior to 1990 were used (latest year of available estimates from data source) (Wisconsin Department of Natural Resources, 2005a, 2005b, 2007). If no well could be identified for a facility it was assumed to be 100 percent supplied by surface water; these sites were verified as being located close to a water body (e.g., stream, wetland, or lake) from an aerial photo or topographic map. For sites with a water source determined but no withdrawal data available, the median value of 0.0264 Mgal/d ground water and 0.0362 Mgal/d surface water for aquacultural water-use permits was applied from the adjacent State of Minnesota's water-use reporting program (Minnesota Department of Natural Resources, 2007) assuming similar water needs. Of the 83 facilities in this compilation, 37 percent had reported water use, 27 percent had the Minnesota median value applied, 24 percent were estimated from high-capacity-well permit data, and 12 percent carried over a water-use estimate from the 2000 compilation.

Table 11.   Livestock water use in Wisconsin, by county, 2005.

[Mgal/d, million gallons per day]

	WITHDRAWALS, in Mgal/d		
County	Ground water	Surface water	Total
Adams	0.16	0.02	0.18
Ashland	.13	.01	.14
Barron	1.44	.16	1.61
Bayfield	.19	.02	.22
Brown	2.00	.22	2.22
Buffalo	1.30	.14	1.44
Burnett	.21	.02	.23
Calumet	1.08	.12	1.20
Chippewa	1.58	.18	1.76
Clark	2.81	.31	3.12
Columbia	1.00	.11	1.12
Crawford	.67	.07	.74
Dane	2.51	.28	2.79
Dodge	2.15	.24	2.39
Door	.43	.05	.47
Douglas	.11	.01	.12
Dunn	1.18	.13	1.31
Eau Claire	.63	.07	.70
Florence	.04	.00	.05
Fond du Lac	1.94	0.22	2.16
Forest	.08	.01	.08
Grant	3.07	.34	3.42
Green	1.60	.18	1.78
Green Lake	.46	.05	.51
Iowa	1.51	.17	1.67
Iron	.02	.00	.02
Jackson	.73	.08	.81
Jefferson	1.10	.12	1.22
Juneau	.45	.05	.50
Kenosha	.19	.02	.22
Kewaunee	1.33	.15	1.48
La Crosse	.62	.07	.69
Lafayette	1.73	.19	1.92
Langlade	.34	.04	.37
Lincoln	.25	.03	.28
Manitowoc	1.96	.22	2.18
Marathon	2.80	.31	3.11

Table 11. Livestock water use in Wisconsin, by county, 2005—Continued.

[Mgal/d, million gallons per day]

County	WITHDRAWALS, in Mgal/d		
	Ground water	Surface water	Total
Marinette	.57	.06	.64
Marquette	.33	.04	.36
Menominee	.04	.00	.04
Milwaukee	.04	.00	.05
Monroe	1.33	.15	1.48
Oconto	.97	.11	1.08
Oneida	.04	.00	.05
Outagamie	1.68	.19	1.86
Ozaukee	.41	.05	.45
Pepin	.46	.05	.52
Pierce	.97	.11	1.07
Polk	.91	.10	1.01
Portage	.74	.08	.83
Price	.23	.03	.26
Racine	.21	.02	.23
Richland	.83	.09	.92
Rock	.83	.09	.92
Rusk	.58	.06	.65
St. Croix	1.20	.13	1.34
Sauk	1.67	.19	1.85
Sawyer	.15	.02	.16
Shawano	1.71	.19	1.90
Sheboygan	1.22	.14	1.36
Taylor	.81	.09	.90
Trempealeau	1.48	.16	1.64
Vernon	1.40	.16	1.55
Vilas	.01	.00	.01
Walworth	.69	.08	.77
Washburn	.21	.02	.23
Washington	.71	.08	.79
Waukesha	.23	.03	.25
Waupaca	1.16	.13	1.29
Waushara	.29	.03	.32
Winnebago	.66	.07	.73
Wood	1.00	.11	1.12
Total	65.57	7.27	72.86

Table 12. Water use for aquaculture in Wisconsin, by county, 2005.

[Mgal/d, million gallons per day]

County	WITHDRAWALS, in Mgal/d			Number of facilities accounted for
	Ground water	Surface water	Total	
Adams	0.08	0.00	0.08	2
Ashland	.00	.60	.60	1
Barron	.00	.04	.04	1
Bayfield	3.86	7.61	11.47	4
Brown	.00	.04	.04	1
Buffalo	.00	.00	.00	0
Burnett	.41	.36	.77	2
Calumet	.00	.00	.00	0
Chippewa	.00	.00	.00	0
Clark	.00	.04	.04	1
Columbia	.28	.00	.28	4
Crawford	.00	.00	.00	0
Dane	2.10	.04	2.14	2
Dodge	.00	.00	.00	0
Door	.36	1.80	2.16	1
Douglas	.05	3.46	3.51	2
Dunn	.39	.00	.39	1
Eau Claire	.00	.00	.00	0
Florence	.00	.00	.00	0
Fond du Lac	0.00	0.00	0.00	0
Forest	.50	.50	1.00	1
Grant	.00	.00	.00	0
Green	.00	.00	.00	0
Green Lake	1.89	.00	1.89	1
Iowa	.00	.00	.00	0
Iron	.00	.00	.00	0
Jackson	.00	.00	.00	0
Jefferson	3.24	.00	3.24	2
Juneau	.00	.00	.00	0
Kenosha	.18	.00	.18	1
Kewaunee	.90	.00	.90	3
La Crosse	1.55	.04	1.59	1
Lafayette	.24	.00	.24	1
Langlade	3.42	13.32	16.74	7
Lincoln	.00	.00	.00	0
Manitowoc	.00	.00	.00	0
Marathon	.43	.00	.43	1

Table 12. Water use for aquaculture in Wisconsin, by county, 2005—Continued.

[Mgal/d, million gallons per day]

County	WITHDRAWALS, in Mgal/d			Number of facilities accounted for
	Ground water	Surface water	Total	
Marinette	1.57	2.55	4.12	2
Marquette	3.61	.36	3.97	4
Menominee	.36	.36	.72	1
Milwaukee	.00	.04	.04	1
Monroe	.12	.00	.12	1
Oconto	.05	.60	.65	1
Oneida	1.70	1.08	2.78	2
Outagamie	.06	.07	.13	4
Ozaukee	.12	.00	.12	1
Pepin	.00	.00	.00	0
Pierce	.00	.00	.00	0
Polk	4.83	.04	4.87	3
Portage	.36	.07	.43	3
Price	.00	.00	.00	0
Racine	.20	1.00	1.20	1
Richland	.00	.00	.00	0
Rock	.00	.00	.00	0
Rusk	.00	.00	.00	0
St Croix	.00	2.20	2.20	2
Sauk	.00	.04	.04	2
Sawyer	.36	.36	.72	1
Shawano	0.00	0.04	0.04	1
Sheboygan	1.65	.40	2.05	4
Taylor	.00	.00	.00	0
Trempealeau	.00	.00	.00	0
Vernon	1.40	.04	1.44	2
Vilas	.50	5.00	5.50	1
Walworth	.75	.00	.75	2
Washburn	.07	1.14	1.21	2
Washington	.00	.00	.00	0
Waukesha	.00	.00	.00	0
Waupaca	.00	.00	.00	0
Waushara	.89	.00	.89	2
Winnebago	.00	.00	.00	0
Wood	.00	.00	.00	0
Total	38.48	43.24	81.72	83

Industrial

Industrial water use includes water used for such purposes as fabrication, processing, washing, and cooling in facilities that manufacture products. Around 80 percent of all industrial water use in Wisconsin comes from self-supplied resources. The types of industrial facilities considered are defined by the Standard Industrial Classification (SIC) codes (e.g., paper mill). The paper- and allied-products industry is the largest overall industrial water user in Wisconsin for both ground water and surface water, followed by self-supplied water use for milling, chemical, and secondary-metal industries. Conversely, the majority of self-supplied industrial establishments identified are related to food and beverage, earthen materials (e.g., concrete and asphalt production), and general manufacturing industries. Figure 8 illustrates the approximate industrial water use and the number of industries identified with a self-supplied water source by county in Wisconsin for 2005.

Total self-supplied industrial water use in Wisconsin for 2005 was 471 Mgal/d, of which about 15 percent (70.9 Mgal/d) was from ground-water sources and about 85 percent (400 Mgal/d) was from surface-water sources (table 2). Table 13 provides the amount of withdrawal for self-supplied industry and the number of industries identified by county but also provides the amount of publicly supplied industrial water delivered to allow for a complete evaluation of overall industrial water use in Wisconsin for 2005. The greatest industrial (self-supplied) water use occurred in Wood County—124 Mgal/d. The largest industrial ground-water use occurred in Portage County (11.5 Mgal/d), and the largest industrial surface-water use occurred in Wood County (123.8 Mgal/d). The majority of industrial water use by subbasin occurred in Castle-Rock, Lower Fox River, Wolf River, and Lake Dubay subbasins (appendix 2). Figure 8 shows the distribution of the 557 self-supplied industrial facilities identified. The majority (478 industries) acquired water from ground-water sources whereas 80 self-supplied

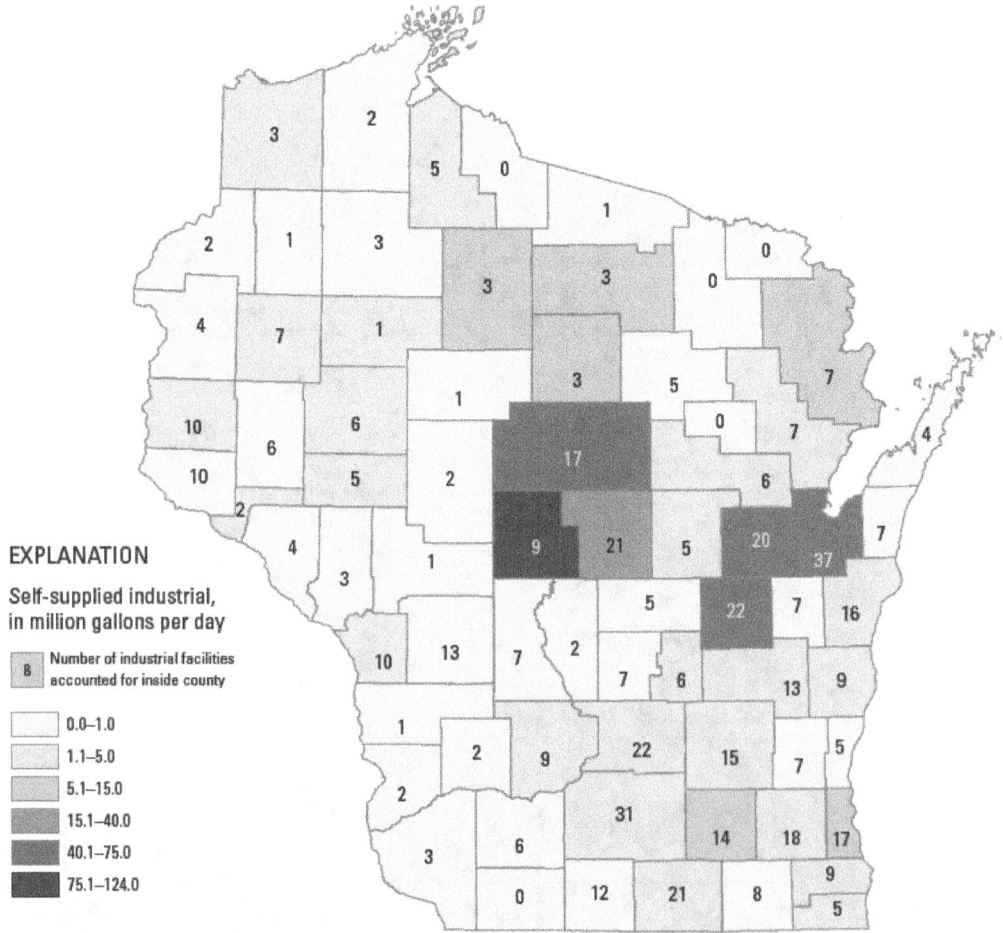

Figure 8. Total self-supplied industrial water use and the approximate number of facilities that have self-supplied water sources in Wisconsin, by county, 2005.

industrial facilities acquired water from surface-water sources (table 13). Brown and Dane Counties have the most industrial sites accounted for (37 and 31 facilities, respectively). Figure 9 illustrates the estimated water use by water source for main industry types in Wisconsin. Most of the surface water withdrawn is used for cooling and is returned, especially for pulp and paper industries, whereas, much of the ground water withdrawn is for processing or product incorporation, especially with food and beverage industries.

A master industry-site list was created from WDNR high-capacity well approvals and surface-wastewater-discharge permits along with archived USGS files. A site or well was categorized according to table 3 called "List of Standard Industrial Classification (SIC) codes by water-use category" of the 2000 guidelines for USGS water-use compilation in the AWUDS (Kenny, 2004). If the type of industrial facility (e.g., paper mill) could not be determined, then water use was described by its intended water-use purpose (e.g., cooling). Most industries do not report water use to the WDNR but do report wastewater discharges. In 2007, under 2003 Wisconsin Act 310, new legislation (Wis. Admin. Code NR 820) was approved that would require owners of high-capacity wells or properties (which includes most self-supplied industries) to report ground-water use annually, but for 2005 these data were not available. Most ground-water-use estimates for self-supplied industries were developed for previous and concurrent USGS investigations at the WI WSC or were obtained from the WDNR Bureau of Drinking Water and Groundwater High-Capacity Well Database (Wisconsin Department of Natural Resources, 2005a). Much of the withdrawal data reflect the average of reported water-use estimates prior to 1990. Most large surface-water industrial users have been identified, and data from 2003 or 2004, when available, were provided from the WDNR (Shaili Pfeiffer, Wisconsin Department of Natural Resources, unpub. data, 2007). Otherwise, when water-use data were not available, the amount of water reported as discharged wastewater[4] was used (although consumptive water use is neglected), and only as a last alternative were estimates from former compilations used. Recently (2007), the WDNR began developing a list of smaller surface-water industrial users (Shaili Pfeiffer, Wisconsin Department of Natural Resources, written commun., 2007), which if available, will be incorporated into the 2010 compilation.

Commercial

Commercial water use includes water used at businesses involved in the sale of goods or services, such as hotels, restaurants, office buildings, hospitals, schools, and civilian and military institutions. The water may be obtained from a public-supply facility or may be self-supplied. In this section, only self-supplied commercial water use is considered. This water-use category has not been required by the NWUIP since 1995 owing to complexities and uncertainties in the water-use estimation. The estimated amount reported is expected to be less than the total commercial water use in Wisconsin as not all self-supplied commercial sites were identified. However, by acknowledging the limitation of using this water-use category estimate, it was reinstated in an effort to restart accounting for all principal water-use categories, to provide a minimum baseline for tracking water use from known sites, and to assess whether trends are emerging. The methodology for estimating self-supplied commercial water use is expected to be refined in 2010.

Self-supplied commercial water use in Wisconsin for 2005 was 10.7 Mgal/d and is assumed to be 100 percent from ground-water sources (table 2). Commercial water use accounts for less than 1 percent of the total water withdrawn in Wisconsin for 2005 whether including or excluding the thermoelectric-power generation water-use category (table 2). A commercial well-inventory approach identified 690 sites with a total of 1,214 ground-water wells. Table 14 provides water-use estimates and a count of how many self-supplied commercial facilities were identified by county in the 2005 compilation. At this time (2009), the number of sites was not identified by subbasin. Table 14 also provides the publicly supplied commercial delivery data to allow for a complete evaluation of known commercial water use in Wisconsin for 2005. The largest self-supplied commercial use of water occurred in Sauk County at 1.14 Mgal/d for 28 sites identified mostly for lodging, resorts, and recreational facilities such as water parks. The Upper Fox River subbasin (07120006) at 0.91 Mgal/d was the largest (appendix 2) while its water use was more for schools, churches, and campgrounds. Although Sauk County had the largest withdrawal, Waukesha County had the most sites with 71 identified.

Commercial businesses do not report water use to the WDNR, although like industry, the 2003 Wisconsin Act 310 (see also Wis. Admin. Code NR 820) would require owners of high-capacity wells or properties (which include several self-supplied commercial sites) to report ground-water use annually. In 2005, most commercial sites and data were based on well approvals on file with the WDNR. As explained under the industrial water-use category, high-capacity wells must have approval by the WDNR; however, some wells that are not high capacity also must be on file with WDNR for public health and safety regulations where water is served to at least 25 individuals daily for at least 60 days of the year (Wis. Admin. Codes NR 811 and NR 812) like a school or restaurant. Therefore, it is possible that several commercial sites may be unaccounted for if they neither operate a high-capacity well nor serve water to the public.

[4]Directly using discharge data is complicated by the fact that the discharged volume may contain both ground- and surface-water sources (Jeffery Ripp, Public Service Commission of Wisconsin, oral commun., 2007) and also may contain a factor of consumptive use. Therefore, most surface-water discharge data from 2000 were used only to compare estimated water use at an industrial facility.

Table 13.   Industrial water use and number of self-supplied industries identified in Wisconsin, by county, 2005.

[Mgal/d, million gallons per day]

| County | WITHDRAWALS, in Mgal/d | | | | Approximate number of self-supplied facilities | | |
| | Self supplied | | | Publicly supplied | | | |
	Ground water	Surface water	Total (self supplied)	Industrial delivery	Using ground water	Using surface water	Total
Adams	0.09	0.00	0.09	0.09	2	0	2
Ashland	.08	2.38	2.46	.07	3	2	5
Barron	1.76	.00	1.76	1.68	7	0	7
Bayfield	.01	.22	.23	.01	1	1	2
Brown	2.87	68.34	71.21	7.97	23	14	37
Buffalo	.36	.00	.36	.05	4	0	4
Burnett	.02	.04	.06	.01	1	1	2
Calumet	.66	.01	.67	1.59	6	1	7
Chippewa	.49	3.53	4.02	2.91	4	2	6
Clark	.18	.00	.18	.33	2	0	2
Columbia	1.61	.00	1.61	.65	22	0	22
Crawford	.35	.00	.35	.45	2	0	2
Dane	3.07	.57	3.64	1.67	31	1	31
Dodge	1.94	.15	2.09	1.34	14	1	15
Door	.16	.00	.16	.19	4	0	4
Douglas	.00	1.03	1.03	.02	0	3	3
Dunn	.89	.00	.89	.58	6	0	6
Eau Claire	0.22	3.12	3.34	1.50	4	1	5
Florence	.00	.00	.00	.00	0	0	0
Fond du Lac	1.52	.00	1.52	1.01	13	0	13
Forest	.00	.00	.00	.02	0	0	0
Grant	.31	.00	.31	.52	3	0	3
Green	.60	.00	.60	.57	12	0	12
Green Lake	1.03	.00	1.03	.48	6	0	6
Iowa	.18	.00	.18	.05	6	0	6
Iron	.00	.00	.00	.01	0	0	0
Jackson	.10	.00	.10	.10	1	0	1
Jefferson	5.99	.00	5.99	1.22	14	0	14
Juneau	.29	.00	.29	.02	7	0	7
Kenosha	.05	1.95	2.00	2.21	3	2	5
Kewaunee	.33	.00	.33	.16	7	0	7
La Crosse	4.64	.00	4.64	2.49	10	0	10
Lafayette	.00	.00	.00	.17	0	0	0
Langlade	.12	.06	.18	.29	4	1	5
Lincoln	.10	7.97	8.07	.15	2	1	3
Manitowoc	.59	1.59	2.18	4.94	14	2	16
Marathon	1.16	41.45	42.61	4.76	13	4	17

Table 13.   Industrial water use and number of self-supplied industries identified in Wisconsin, by county, 2005—Continued.

[Mgal/d, million gallons per day]

| County | WITHDRAWALS, in Mgal/d | | | | Approximate number of self-supplied facilities | | |
| | Self supplied | | | Publicly supplied | | | |
	Ground water	Surface water	Total (self supplied)	Industrial delivery	Using ground water	Using surface water	Total
Marinette	1.49	8.67	10.16	1.91	3	4	7
Marquette	.45	.00	.45	.00	7	0	7
Menominee	.00	.00	.00	.05	0	0	0
Milwaukee	3.57	6.58	10.15	20.96	10	7	17
Monroe	.73	.00	.73	.49	13	0	13
Oconto	.25	2.54	2.79	.54	4	3	7
Oneida	.35	8.47	8.82	.45	2	1	3
Outagamie	2.18	45.57	47.75	2.21	13	7	20
Ozaukee	.62	.00	.62	1.56	5	0	5
Pepin	.02	1.25	1.27	.00	1	1	2
Pierce	.72	.00	.72	.06	10	0	10
Polk	.38	.00	.38	.94	4	0	4
Portage	11.51	14.67	26.18	4.62	19	2	21
Price	.65	6.10	6.75	.58	1	2	3
Racine	.90	2.90	3.80	8.17	8	1	9
Richland	.29	.00	.29	.53	2	0	2
Rock	3.13	.00	3.13	5.34	21	0	21
Rusk	.00	1.37	1.37	.05	0	1	1
St Croix	1.14	.00	1.14	.36	10	0	10
Sauk	1.51	.00	1.51	2.93	9	0	9
Sawyer	.08	.00	.08	.08	3	0	3
Shawano	.15	2.90	3.05	.77	5	1	6
Sheboygan	2.06	.00	2.06	8.37	9	0	9
Taylor	.04	.00	.04	.16	1	0	1
Trempealeau	.22	.00	.22	1.11	3	0	3
Vernon	.03	.00	.03	.16	1	0	1
Vilas	.01	.00	.01	.00	1	0	1
Walworth	.80	.00	.80	1.24	8	0	8
Washburn	.07	.00	.07	.01	1	0	1
Washington	.19	.00	.19	.84	7	0	7
Waukesha	1.24	.32	1.56	2.17	17	1	18
Waupaca	.65	1.00	1.65	3.42	4	1	5
Waushara	.23	.00	.23	.31	5	0	5
Winnebago	3.32	41.44	44.76	2.66	16	6	22
Wood	.18	123.77	123.95	1.02	4	5	9
Total	70.93	399.96	470.89	114.35	478	80	557

A. Ground water

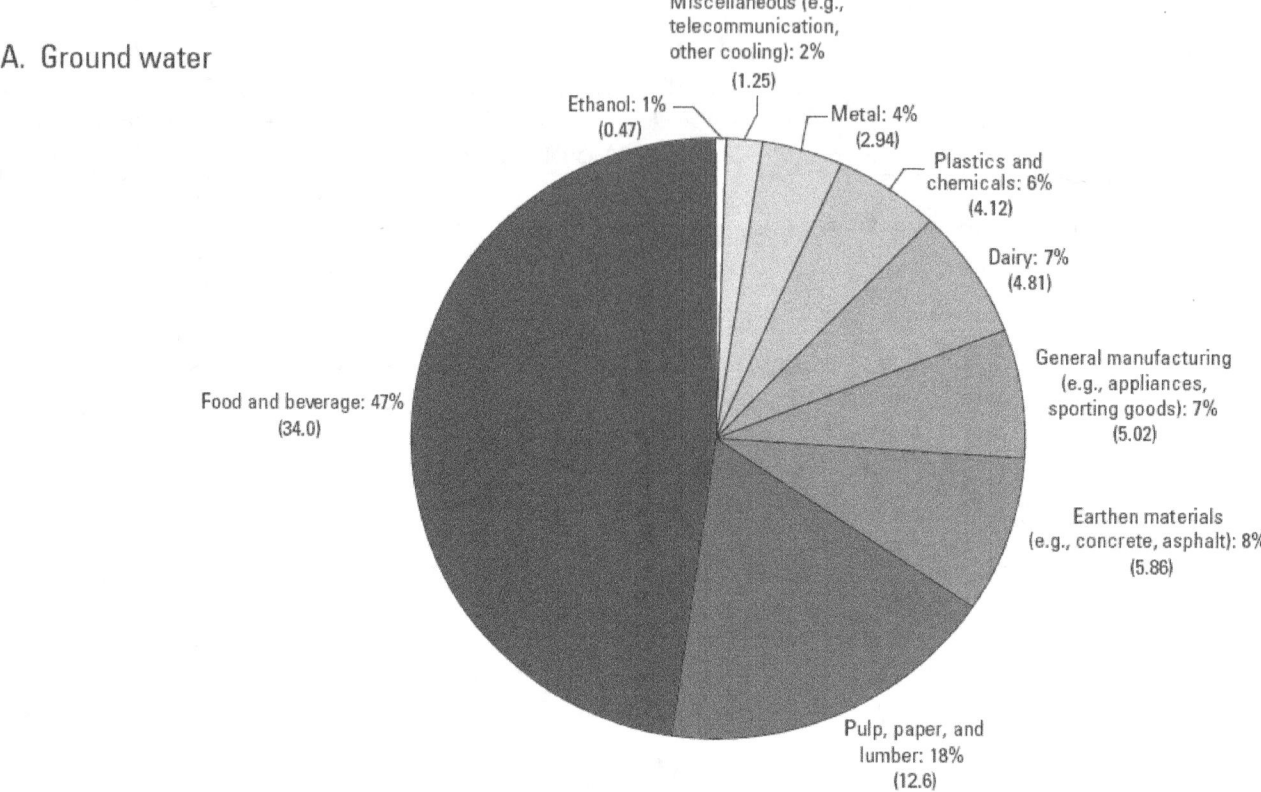

B. Surface water

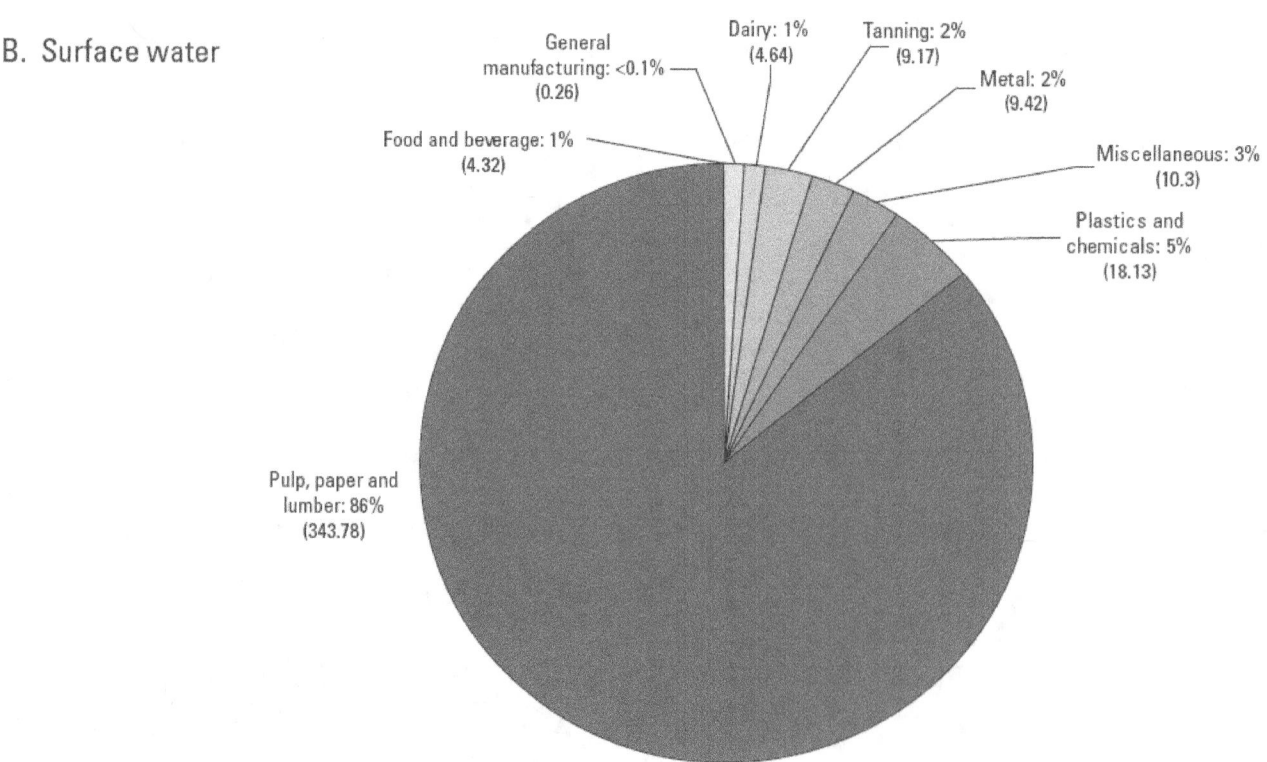

Figure 9.   Estimated water use, by water source, for main industry types in Wisconsin, 2005. (Value inside parenthesis is the amount of water in million gallons per day.)

Table 14. Commercial water use and the number of self-supplied commercial businesses accounted for in Wisconsin, by county, 2005.

[Mgal/d, million gallons per day; --, no water-use sites were identified and no estimate was provided; all surface-water withdrawals are assumed to be zero and have been removed from the table.]

County	WITHDRAWALS, in Mgal/d		Approximate number of self-supplied facilities
	Self supplied	Public supply	
	Ground water	Commercial delivery	
Adams	0.20	0.08	7
Ashland	.00	.27	1
Barron	.03	.52	9
Bayfield	.12	.08	3
Brown	.43	6.26	10
Buffalo	.02	.07	4
Burnett	.04	.09	7
Calumet	.01	.62	4
Chippewa	.04	1.05	6
Clark	.00	.19	1
Columbia	.10	.86	13
Crawford	.03	.34	2
Dane	.38	13.56	28
Dodge	.04	.87	11
Door	.17	.4	21
Douglas	.03	.26	6
Dunn	.02	.35	4
Eau Claire	.07	1.71	7
Florence	.01	.03	2
Fond du Lac	.13	1.25	13
Forest	--	.07	--
Grant	.01	.51	3
Green	.03	.49	4
Green Lake	.44	.22	6
Iowa	.17	.18	8
Iron	--	.09	--
Jackson	.01	.34	2
Jefferson	.08	.9	13
Juneau	.14	.4	6
Kenosha	.13	4.23	20
Kewaunee	.01	.11	4
La Crosse	.79	3.96	19
Lafayette	.03	.1	3
Langlade	.04	.21	4
Lincoln	.03	.26	3
Manitowoc	.26	1.25	10
Marathon	.12	1.89	12

Table 14. Commercial water use and the number of self-supplied commercial businesses accounted for in Wisconsin, by county, 2005—Continued.

[Mgal/d, million gallons per day; --, no water-use sites were identified and no estimate was provided; all surface-water withdrawals are assumed to be zero and have been removed from the table.]

| County | WITHDRAWALS, in Mgal/d | | Approximate number of self-supplied facilities |
| | Self supplied | Public supply | |
	Ground water	Commercial delivery	
Marinette	.02	.42	6
Marquette	0.02	0.04	7
Menominee	.00	.05	1
Milwaukee	.66	29.22	17
Monroe	.29	.46	10
Oconto	.11	.2	8
Oneida	.05	.35	10
Outagamie	.26	2.76	10
Ozaukee	.30	.59	18
Pepin	.01	.08	2
Pierce	.01	.42	3
Polk	.01	.45	2
Portage	.08	1.26	12
Price	.01	.14	2
Racine	.09	3.76	14
Richland	.06	.28	5
Rock	.35	3.02	16
Rusk	.00	.09	1
St Croix	.06	.89	9
Sauk	1.14	2.01	28
Sawyer	.10	.21	4
Shawano	.03	.45	7
Sheboygan	.19	1.67	21
Taylor	--	.08	--
Trempealeau	.03	.31	3
Vernon	.01	.23	4
Vilas	.07	.14	10
Walworth	.53	1.65	32
Washburn	.04	.15	5
Washington	.21	1.43	25
Waukesha	.90	7.25	71
Waupaca	.12	.5	8
Waushara	.35	.53	21
Winnebago	.07	1.76	13
Wood	.32	1.38	9
Total	10.66	108.3	690

From these approval records, a water-use purpose was determined for most well records by the well, owner, or operator names; permit-classification type; or from comments provided within the well-construction report. The well name noted in the record often provided phrases such as clubhouse, boiler room, nature center, snow making, main supply, or standby, which provided a way to identify the water purpose of the well. Well names helped to omit wells where water use was assumed negligible like a hand-pump well at a campground or where a water-use estimate was too uncertain, such as with most maintenance shops, rural churches, small stores and offices, and municipal airports.

Thermoelectric-Power Generation

Withdrawals for thermoelectric-power generation include self-supplied water used in the generation of electrical power with fossil-fuel and nuclear energy. This category excludes water used for domestic purposes or fire-protection supplies at power-generation facilities. Most of the water withdrawn for thermoelectric-power generation is used for heat removal by a cooling system. In 2005, only one power plant was known to have a closed cooling system in which water is withdrawn from a source, circulated through heat exchangers, cooled, and then recycled; all others were assumed to have once-through cooling systems in which water is withdrawn from a source, circulated through heat exchangers, and returned to a surface-water body. Other water uses include plant service water (for different heat exchanges or plant systems), fly-ash control, and an emergency cooling supply. One major revision in the 2005 compilation is the inclusion of several newly identified facilities (mostly privately owned) generating their own thermoelectric power.

Thermoelectric water use is the largest use of water in Wisconsin and also in the United States (Hutson and others, 2004). This category usually accounts for 70 to 85 percent of the total water withdrawn in Wisconsin, though, much of this water is returned. In 2005, 80.1 percent of the total water used was for thermoelectric-power generation of which 99.95 percent (6,895 Mgal/d) was from surface-water sources. Industrial facilities that generate thermoelectric power are called combined heat-and-power plant (or cogeneration) facilities. If the data provided from the industrial facility are sufficient to identify water used in power generation, that amount of water and the power generated are compiled with other county thermoelectric-power water-use data. In 2005, 56 facilities were identified and estimated to have generated 56,561 gWh of thermoelectric energy for all application categories (public energy, pulp and paper, wood, and facility energy). Lake Michigan subbasin supplies the source water for over one-half (or 53.3 percent) of the total power generated. Water from 20 other subbasins constituted the remaining

water used, and data are shown in appendix 3. Table 15 shows thermoelectric-power generation and water-use data for the 28 counties estimated with such facilities. Ground-water use for thermoelectric-power generation was less than 1 percent of total water withdrawn in 2005 (3.37 Mgal/d). Milwaukee and Wood Counties had the most thermoelectric-power generating facilities identified; however, Milwaukee County generated 8.5 times more energy from power plants and facilities than did Wood County from pulp and paper mills.

Precisely one-half of the 56 facilities identified had current energy production data available from the PSC, which collects data on municipal power-generation plants that produce more than 10 Megawatts per year. For the remaining facilities, energy data either were obtained from U.S. Department of Energy–Energy Information Administration (2004a, 2004b) or a coefficient-based approach based on power-generation-capacity data listed at the Energy and Environmental Analysis, Inc. (2007) website. Water-use estimates were calculated in one of three ways:

1. from past production and withdrawal data;

2. from WDNR surface-water discharge volumes measured in 2000 (although consumptive water use is neglected); or

3. from a default water-use equation for thermoelectric-power generation—*Total estimated water use = Production data, in gWh χ water requirement of 15 Mgal/d to generate 1 gWh*—where 15 Mgal/d was the median value calculated from records that had both water-use and energy-production data.

Mining

Mining water use in Wisconsin includes water that is used for the extraction of minerals and ores. The category includes quarrying, milling, and other operations done as part of the mining activity, such as dust control or dewatering (removal of water through draining or pumping to lower the water table), but does not include water used for washing and sorting or concrete and asphalt operations. The latter uses are considered industrial water use although mines and processing plants are sometimes co-located, and water used for mining is not easily discernible from water used for processing (Kenny, 2004).

Prior to 1985, mining withdrawals were included with the industrial water-use estimate. In 2000, water used for mining was not estimated. For the 2005 compilation, mining water-use estimates were provided by county and subbasin from the NWUIP, which were based on coefficients derived from various sources including U.S. Census Bureau and U.S. Bureau of Mines reports.

Table 15. Thermoelectric-power generation and water use in Wisconsin, by county, 2005.

[Mgal/d, Million gallons per day; gWh, gigawatthour(s) of energy produced]

County	WITHDRAWALS, in Mgal/d			Power generated (gWh)	Number of facilities accounted for using ground water	Number of facilities accounted for using surface water
	Ground water	Surface water	Total			
Adams	0.00	0.00	0.00	0.00	0	0
Ashland	.00	50.56	50.56	337.08	0	1
Barron	.00	.00	.00	.00	0	0
Bayfield	.00	.00	.00	.00	0	0
Brown	.00	413.38	413.38	2,890.30	0	3
Buffalo	.66	532.50	533.16	3,710.27	1	2
Burnett	.00	.00	.00	.00	0	0
Calumet	.00	.00	.00	.00	0	0
Chippewa	.00	.00	.00	.00	0	0
Clark	.00	.00	.00	.00	0	0
Columbia	.50	18.00	18.50	6,698.54	1	1
Crawford	.00	.00	.00	.00	0	0
Dane	.00	226.69	226.69	1,260.25	0	4
Dodge	.00	1.97	1.97	13.14	0	1
Door	.00	.00	.00	.00	0	0
Douglas	.00	.00	.00	.00	0	0
Dunn	.00	.00	.00	.00	0	0
Eau Claire	.00	.00	.00	.00	0	0
Florence	.00	.00	.00	.00	0	0
Fond du Lac	.00	.00	.00	.00	0	0
Forest	.00	.00	.00	.00	0	0
Grant	.04	255.94	255.98	1,470.08	1	2
Green	.00	.00	.00	.00	0	0
Green Lake	.00	.00	.00	.00	0	0
Iowa	.00	.00	.00	.00	0	0
Iron	.00	.00	.00	.00	0	0
Jackson	.00	.00	.00	.00	0	0
Jefferson	.00	2.59	2.59	140.17	0	1
Juneau	.00	.00	.00	.00	0	0
Kenosha	.00	9.05	9.05	8,459.99	0	1
Kewaunee	.01	823.62	823.63	3,873.88	1	1
La Crosse	.42	42.16	42.58	77.10	1	3
Lafayette	.00	.00	.00	.00	0	0
Langlade	.00	.00	.00	.00	0	0
Lincoln	.00	1.45	1.45	9.66	0	1
Manitowoc	1.01	2,122.13	2,123.14	7,225.66	1	2
Marathon	.45	163.55	164.00	3,629.26	1	3

Table 15. Thermoelectric-power generation and water use in Wisconsin, by county, 2005—Continued.

[Mgal/d, Million gallons per day; gWh, gigawatthour(s) of energy produced]

County	WITHDRAWALS, in Mgal/d			Power generated (gWh)	Number of facilities accounted for using ground water	Number of facilities accounted for using surface water
	Ground water	Surface water	Total			
Marinette	.00	26.19	26.19	243.37	0	2
Marquette	.00	.00	.00	.00	0	0
Menominee	0.00	0.00	0.00	0.00	0	0
Milwaukee	.00	1,075.17	1,075.17	7,439.34	0	5
Monroe	.00	.00	.00	.00	0	0
Oconto	.00	.00	.00	.00	0	0
Oneida	.00	15.77	15.77	105.12	0	1
Outagamie	.00	33.01	33.01	220.05	0	3
Ozaukee	.00	291.42	291.42	511.55	1	1
Pepin	.00	.00	.00	.00	0	0
Pierce	.00	.00	.00	.00	0	0
Polk	.00	.00	.00	.00	0	0
Portage	.00	7.03	7.03	46.87	0	2
Price	.00	3.74	3.74	24.97	0	1
Racine	.00	.00	.00	.00	0	0
Richland	.00	.00	.00	.00	0	0
Rock	.12	50.00	50.12	395.03	1	3
Rusk	.00	.00	.00	.00	0	0
St Croix	.00	.82	.82	5.48	0	1
Sauk	.00	.00	.00	.00	0	0
Sawyer	.00	.00	.00	.00	0	0
Shawano	.00	.00	.00	.00	0	0
Sheboygan	.01	377.18	377.19	4,294.72	1	1
Taylor	.00	.00	.00	.00	0	0
Trempealeau	.00	.00	.00	.00	0	0
Vernon	.15	209.79	209.94	2,540.59	1	1
Vilas	.00	.44	.44	2.96	0	1
Walworth	.00	.00	.00	.00	0	0
Washburn	.00	.00	.00	.00	0	0
Washington	.00	.00	.00	.00	0	0
Waukesha	.00	.00	.00	.00	0	0
Waupaca	.00	.00	.00	.00	0	0
Waushara	.00	.00	.00	.00	0	0
Winnebago	.00	10.32	10.32	68.82	0	3
Wood	.00	130.09	130.09	867.24	0	5
Total	3.37	6,894.56	6,897.93	5,6561.49	11	56

There are an estimated 2,500 to 3,000 nonmetallic-mine sites (sand-and-gravel and crushed-stone operations) in Wisconsin, and presently, there are no metal mines in operation (Wisconsin Department of Natural Resources, 2004). Mining water use totaled 32.5 Mgal/d of which about 54 percent (17.6 Mgal/d) was from ground-water sources and about 46 percent (14.9 Mgal/d) was from surface-water sources (table 2). In 2005, mining withdrawals were less than 1 percent of total water withdrawn or 1.9 percent of the total excluding thermoelectric water use. Some of the more populated counties had the highest mining water use; in fact, the top three counties of use (Walworth, Waukesha, and Racine) are located in southeastern Wisconsin (table 16). Mining withdrawals in 2005 were about 246 percent (14.9 Mgal/d) greater for surface water and 122 percent (17.6 Mgal/d) greater for ground water than in 1995, when water use was last estimated, largely owing to the shift in estimation methodology.

Table 16.   Mining water use in Wisconsin, by county, 2005.

[Mgal/d, million gallons per day; data were provided by U.S. Geological Survey National Water Use Information Program]

County	WITHDRAWALS, in Mgal/d		
	Ground water	Surface water	Total
Adams	0.00	0.00	0.00
Ashland	.02	.02	.04
Barron	.25	.00	.25
Bayfield	.88	.00	.88
Brown	.41	.37	.78
Buffalo	.00	.00	.00
Burnett	.08	.07	.15
Calumet	.01	.00	.01
Chippewa	.30	.27	.57
Clark	.20	.18	.38
Columbia	.18	.16	.34
Crawford	.03	.03	.06
Dane	.00	1.60	1.60
Dodge	.33	.30	.63
Door	.13	.12	.25
Douglas	.14	.13	.27
Dunn	.01	.01	.02
Eau Claire	.08	.07	.15
Florence	.03	.02	.05
Fond du Lac	.19	.17	.36
Forest	.05	.04	.09
Grant	.14	.13	.27
Green	.03	.03	.06
Green Lake	.82	.74	1.56
Iowa	.02	.02	.04
Iron	.02	.02	.04
Jackson	.40	.00	.40
Jefferson	.09	.09	.18
Juneau	.44	.40	.84
Kenosha	.20	.18	.38
Kewaunee	.04	.04	.08
La Crosse	.96	.87	1.83

Table 16. Mining water use in Wisconsin, by county, 2005—Continued.

[Mgal/d, million gallons per day; data were provided by U.S. Geological Survey National Water Use Information Program]

County	WITHDRAWALS, in Mgal/d		
	Ground water	Surface water	Total
Lafayette	.03	.03	.06
Langlade	.27	.25	.52
Lincoln	.06	.06	.12
Manitowoc	.57	.52	1.09
Marathon	.44	.40	.84
Marinette	.10	.09	.19
Marquette	.00	.00	.00
Menominee	.00	.00	.00
Milwaukee	0.22	0.20	0.42
Monroe	.19	.17	.36
Oconto	.18	.16	.34
Oneida	.07	.06	.13
Outagamie	.61	.55	1.16
Ozaukee	.19	.17	.36
Pepin	.00	.00	.00
Pierce	.13	.12	.25
Polk	.34	.31	.65
Portage	.58	.00	.58
Price	.01	.01	.02
Racine	1.02	.92	1.94
Richland	.04	.04	.08
Rock	.44	.40	.84
Rusk	.16	.15	.31
St Croix	.58	.52	1.10
Sauk	.23	.21	.44
Sawyer	.02	.01	.03
Shawano	.04	.03	.07
Sheboygan	.18	.16	.34
Taylor	.47	.43	.90
Trempealeau	.08	.07	.15
Vernon	.01	.01	.02
Vilas	.02	.02	.04
Walworth	1.36	1.24	2.60
Washburn	.01	.00	.01
Washington	.75	.00	.75
Waukesha	1.35	1.22	2.57
Waupaca	.14	.12	.26
Waushara	.01	.01	.02
Winnebago	.09	.08	.17
Wood	.12	.11	.23
Total	17.59	14.93	32.52

Assumptions and Limitations

This compilation describes select off-stream water uses and excludes in-stream water uses, such as water used for transportation, recreation, or producing hydroelectricity. The 2005 Wisconsin water-use compilation did not quantify consumptive water use (e.g., reservoir evapotranspiration), conveyance loss, return flows, wastewater treatment, reclaimed wastewater, and water use for remediation. It is acknowledged that assistance is needed from the NWUIP to improve quality assurance and control of such estimates and to determine guidance and standards for methodologies for such assessments (National Research Council, 2002).

Data reported to the WDNR include errors in basic well information, such as well status, owner or operator name(s), and (or) well-construction details; water-use estimates prior to 1990 may be inaccurate (William Furbish and Jeffrey Helmuth, Wisconsin Department of Natural Resources, personal commun(s)., 2004). Water use may be either over or underestimated when using obsolete data or data of questionable quality to create water-use estimates. Most water-use estimates based on well inventories containing water-use data prior to 1990 (mostly industrial and commercial water-use categories) were compared to well withdrawals for similar water-use purposes as reported to the MNDNR Water Appropriations Permit Program; however, these estimates will be re-evaluated for the 2010 compilation, in accordance with the 2003 Wisconsin Act 310, in light of much high-capacity well withdrawal data collected as of 2007.

Certain water-use categories included assumptions as part of the water-use estimation methodology. In 2005, public-supply water use was the only category required to be reported by the State of Wisconsin; therefore, confidence is high in these water-use estimates. Alternatively, none of the self-supplied water-use categories were required to be reported, and as a result, there is less confidence in these water-use estimates. Future compilations should improve with current and forthcoming methodologies when more timely means are possible; therefore, comparisons to former compilations should allow for changes in methods or data sources that may occur.

For public supply, it has not been determined which public-supply water utilities provide a portion of their withdrawn water to power-generation facilities. It is likely that there are a few but presently (2009) that water is defined under the industrial-meter classification for public-supply delivery. Not all public water-supply systems were identified, such as those for mobile-home parks, subdivisions, correctional institutions, or military installations. It was assumed that the entire population was served for a city or village that had a water-supply system. It also was assumed that the housing percent correction for three or more units in a single structure was reasonable to correct for that portion of commercially delivered water that was ultimately for domestic water-use purposes.

Water use for self-supplied industrial and commercial may be either over or underestimated owing to changes in production or when wells have been sold to another industry or business with differing water needs. Water use may be overestimated if the water-use default was too great, water-conservation measures were applied, the facility had closed, a well was abandoned, water supply switched to public-supply delivery, or using water-use data prior to 1990 that reflected a peak in water requirements. Water use may be underestimated if the water-use default was too conservative, not all the industrial wells were accounted for, an industry was missed, or water-use data prior to 1990 did not yet peak in its water requirements.

Additionally, no self-supplied commercial water-use data were collected for 2000 so the values reported in the table called "Water Use by County, 2000" (Ellefson and others, 2002) were estimated based on a percent delivery from the public-supply total withdrawal and may not be comparable for compilation years proceeding and following. Water for commercial use was assumed to be potable and therefore 100 percent from ground water, but it is possible that some commercial businesses may withdraw surface water to meet their water needs.

Some self-supplied domestic per-capita-use coefficients derived were lower than expected especially in counties where there are few public-supply-water systems or where population density was low. The self-supplied per-capita-use estimates were based upon a corrected estimate for public-supply domestic deliveries. Domestic water use was assumed to be 100 percent from ground water, but it is possible that homes may have access to surface water, such as from a spring, and use this water.

Statewide water-use data and estimates have been compiled for Wisconsin every 5 years since 1950, and during this 55-year period data-collection techniques, sources of information, and water-use estimation methods were periodically re-evaluated and revised or changed leaving historical water-use values sometimes difficult to assess. In addition, when water-use data are only compiled on 5-year intervals, any unique circumstance can influence the values for that year and make comparing trends difficult (Marella, 2004).

For example, comparison among the 2005 compilation and previous compilations presents complications in that methodologies have shifted over the last few compilations. For golf course irrigation, it was assumed in the 2005 compilation that all courses irrigate to some degree. For crop irrigation, the 1,000 (gal/d)/acre water-application coefficient used in the 2005 compilation may be too high for much of the State especially for particular counties where there are fewer principal crops, such as corn, soybeans, or potatoes, but rather specialty crops such as mushrooms, mint, or orchards. The 2005 compilation was the first instance where a permit-based method was applied to estimate surface-water withdrawals for irrigation. Irrigation water use is the largest category of self-supplied water use (387 Mgal/d), and the reported 2005 estimate is believed to be at the higher end of the range of possible irrigation water use. To date (2009), no water-use compilation in Wisconsin has taken into account irrigation variables, but the methodology will be revised for the 2010 compilation to better reflect crop type, topography, soil type, and climate for each county or subbasin.

Eight subbasins (Pensaukee River, Lower Fox River, Lake Winnebago, Manitowoc-Sheboygan Rivers, Pike-Root Rivers, Milwaukee River, Upper Rock River, and Lower Rock River subbasins) had significant revisions to their boundaries, which altered the amount of land and population within the subbasin and hence the percent contribution from that and adjacent subbasins. Because most water-use estimates by subbasin are based on the percent contribution of the comprising counties and not site data, there is a distributive effect that may not accurately reflect land use within specific county contributions. Additionally, some previously assigned water-use sites may have been reassigned into different subbasins, and some past water-use estimates prior to 2000 for industry and thermoelectric power were improperly compiled for where the water was used rather than for where the water was withdrawn (a deviation from NWUIP standards). Therefore, a comparison of these eight subbasins and their adjacent subbasins among the 2005 compilation and previous compilations would be less accurate.

The source for population-density data also was revised in the 2005 compilation. In previous compilations, the WI WSC used U.S. Census Bureau data for population density, but during the 2005 effort it was found to inaccurately describe areas around the perimeters of Wisconsin or where there are significant areas of wetlands; therefore, population density was recalculated with higher resolution geographic information system datasets of land cover, county boundaries, and watershed delineations (Multi-Resolution Land Characteristics Consortium, 2001; Wisconsin Department of Natural Resources, 1998; U.S. Department of Agriculture–Natural Resources Conservation Service, 2008).

Trends in Water Use, 1950–2005

USGS water-use compilation began in 1950 for the State of Wisconsin and has continued every 5 years until the most recent compilation for 2005, with the exception of 1980 that was compiled for 1979 instead. Table 17 shows that the total amount of water being used in Wisconsin increases with population growth. The population in 1950 was around 3.43 million persons and in 2005 was estimated at 5.54 million persons (U.S. Census Bureau, 2006, 2008). Population during this 55-year time period has risen 61.5 percent. Total water use for Wisconsin in 1950 was estimated at 2,079 Mgal/d and over the past 55 years has increased four times to 8,608 Mgal/d. Total ground-water use from 1950 to 2005 increased from

297 to 986 Mgal/d, an increase of about 232 percent. Total surface-water use from 1950 to 2005 increased from 1,783 to 7,622 Mgal/d, an increase of 328 percent. Figure 10 shows that ground-water use has increased steadily with population growth from 1950 to 2005. Surface-water and total water use, although they have increased during the same time period, were affected by the amount of surface water withdrawn for thermoelectric-power and industrial water-use purposes, which more drastically fluctuate. Comparing the 5-year water-use totals from the 1950–2005 compilations, on average, total water use increased 5.7 percent, ground-water use increased 4.2 percent, and surface-water use increased 6.0 percent.

Table 18 and figure 11 show a breakdown of water use by select water-use categories. Thermoelectric power, mining, and aquacultural water uses have been removed from the total; commercial water use, first estimated in 1979, has been included. Of the selected water-use categories, public supply has been and continues to be the largest water use in Wisconsin. Public supply had increased rather steadily until 1990 and appeared to be stabilizing if not declining as shown for 2005. Irrigation water use increased with each compilation as did irrigated acreage reported in the Census of Agriculture reports for Wisconsin. The notable doubling of irrigation water use, in 2005, was largely caused by a switch in the estimation method applied. The new method, based on a single coefficient, is believed to be more accurate for certain crops like potatoes and corn, but likely overestimates irrigation for other crops like sod and fruit. Refinements will continue for estimates in this category. Industrial water use peaked between 1980 and 1990 and has stabilized although there have been shifts on a more local scale (e.g., specific counties). For example, industrial withdrawals have been growing in parts of central Wisconsin for new growth industries, such as ethanol production, while in southeastern Wisconsin industrial water use has been declining from the closures of several early industries (metal foundries, tanneries, and breweries). The full extent of commercial water use in Wisconsin is unknown; however, it is expected to be minor as many businesses identified in WDNR databases as having high-capacity ground-water wells or serving water to the public owing to health-regulation requirements have been accounted for. Self-supplied domestic and livestock water uses were combined under a past water-use category called "rural supply" for the 1950 –1975 compilations. Beginning with the 1979 compilation, self-supplied domestic and livestock water uses were reported separately. Livestock water use peaked in the 1985 compilation, whereas domestic water use peaked in 2000. In figure 11, self-supplied domestic and livestock water-use estimates since 1979 were recombined under the former "rural supply" category to compare with former compilations; aquacultural water use was not incorporated. In 2005, 54.5 percent of the rural-supply withdrawal is for domestic water-use purposes.

Table 17. Water use by water source and total population in Wisconsin, 1950–2005.

[Population in thousands of persons; water use in million gallons per day; thermoelectric, thermoelectric-power generation]

Water source	1950	1955	1960	1965	1970	1975	1979	1985	1990	1995	2000	2005
Ground-water use	296.79	346.60	522.30	648.00	493.00	458.00	602.82	575.08	666.22	783.20	839.94	985.91
Surface-water use	1,782.68	4,716.40	3,776.00	4,447.00	5,825.00	5,726.00	5,203.76	6,160.49	5,806.18	6,488.22	6,186.95	7,622.15
Total use	2,079.47	5,063.00	4,298.30	5,095.00	6,318.00	6,184.00	5,806.58	6,735.57	6,472.40	7,271.42	7,625.76	8,608.06
Total use excluding thermoelectric	479.47	563.00	928.30	935.00	1,018.00	984.00	1,153.34	1,292.40	1,376.44	1,443.46	1,631.32	1,710.13
Population	3,434.58	3,693.18	3,951.78	4,184.75	4,417.73	4,561.75	4,705.64	4,804.49	4,891.76	5,102.47	5,363.71	5,536.20

Note: Totals do not necessarily equal the sum of parts or may not be comparable to other table totals because of rounding.

Table 18. Total water use by select water-use categories, in Wisconsin, 1950–2005.

[Water use in million gallons per day; "--", data not available; thermoelectric, thermoelectric, thermoelectric-power generation]

Select water-use categories	1950	1955	1960	1965	1970	1975	1979	1985	1990	1995	2000	2005
Public supply	290.0	330.0	370.0	450.0	490.0	460.0	563.3	575.3	595.3	599.8	623.2	552.4
Irrigation	4.5	9.0	15.3	39.0	53.0	71.0	85.6	89.4	145.8	191.4	225.6	401.8
Industrial	75.0	120.0	230.0	291.0	330.0	312.0	418.0	451.4	434.9	435.0	450.9	470.9
Commercial	--	--	--	--	--	--	9.0	10.0	10.7	15.7	20.0	10.7
Rural supply (domestic & livestock)	110.0	104.0	143.0	155.0	145.0	147.0	149.0	172.2	158.4	156.0	162.6	160.2
Subtotal of select water-use categories	479.5	563.0	758.3	935.0	1,018.0	990.0	1,224.9	1,298.3	1,345.1	1,397.9	1,482.3	1,596.0
Subtotal of other water uses[a]	1,600.0	4,500.0	3,540.0	4,160.0	5,300.0	5,194.0	4,581.7	5,437.3	5,174.1	5,873.5	6,144.6	7,012.2

[a]Other water uses include mining, aquaculture, thermoelectric, and commercial water uses when these data became available. The majority of the other water uses subtotal is for thermoelectric; however, other water use prior to 1979 was exclusively attributed to thermoelectric.

Note: Totals do not necessarily equal the sum of parts or may not be comparable to other table totals because of rounding.

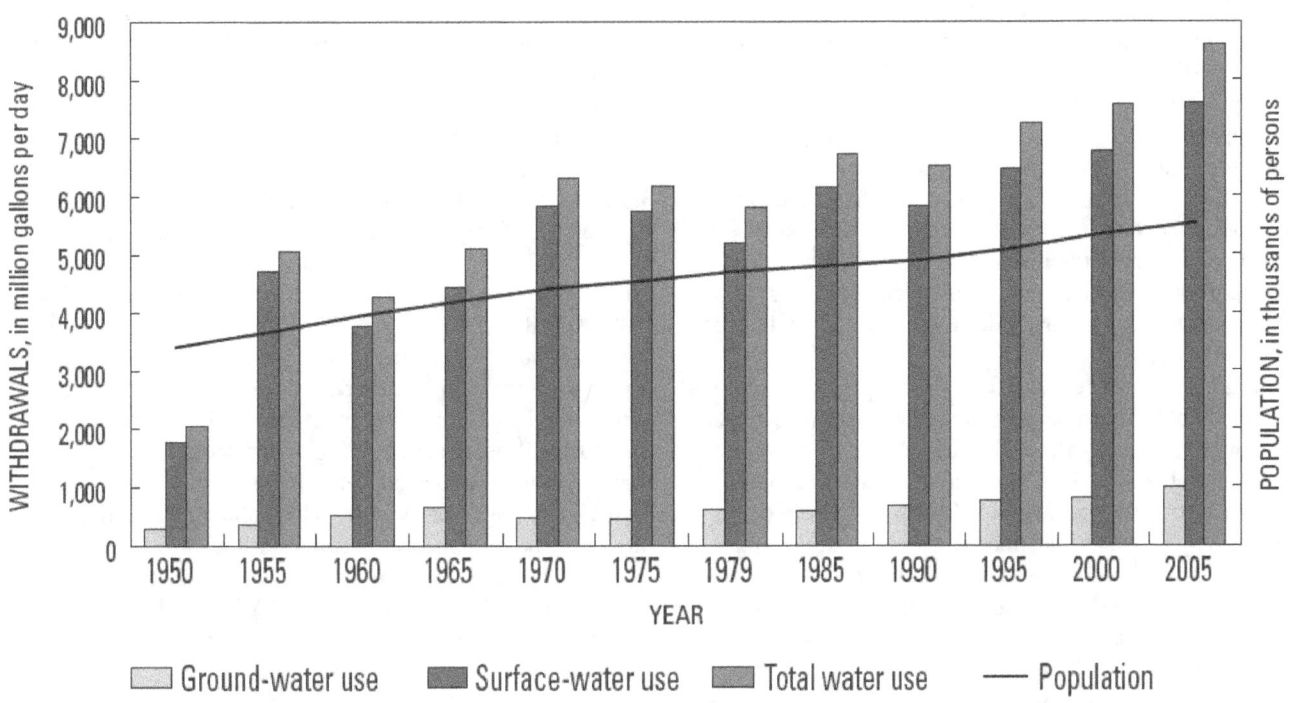

Figure 10. Total population and water use, including thermoelectric-power generation, by water source for Wisconsin, 1950–2005. (Figure 10 corresponds with table 17).

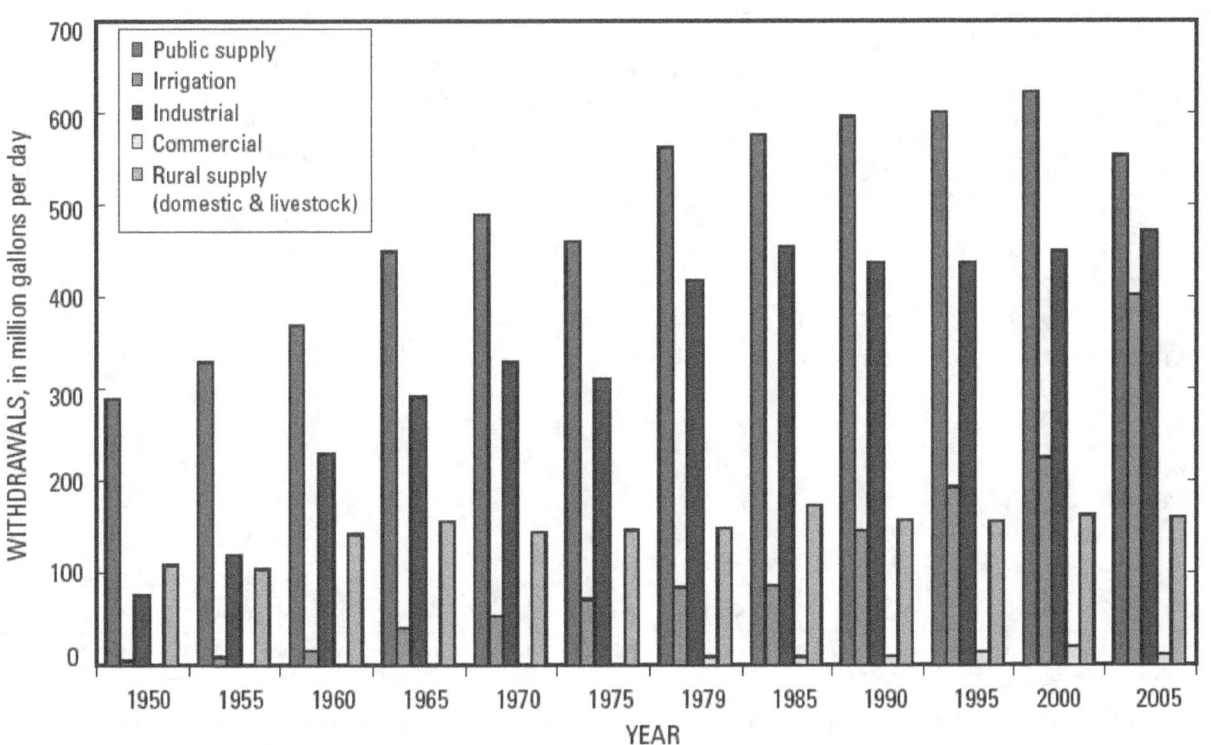

Figure 11. Total water use by select water-use categories, in Wisconsin, 1950–2005. (Water-use categories not graphed include mining, aquaculture, thermoelectric power, and commercial (1950–1975); much of these data were not compiled prior to 1985.)

Per-capita use is described for total water use of select categories, public-supply water use, and domestic water use from 1950 to 2005 (table 19). Figure 12a shows the various types of per-capita use analyzed with respect to each other. Public-supply water use had ultimately driven the pattern of water use until the 1980s when irrigation, and to a lesser degree industrial water uses, continued to outpace the growth of public-supply water use (table 18). Figure 12b compares the State population to total water use for most categories excluding thermoelectric, mining, and aquaculture. As population increases so usually does development and hence more water is used.

Ground and surface water for public supply had increased at about the same percentage rate until 1979 when the amount of surface-water withdrawn stabilized at around 300 Mgal/d (table 20). Ground-water withdrawals continued to increase until peaking in 2000 at 293 Mgal/d. Public-supply per-capita use has declined since 1985, although the population served has increased (fig. 12c). From 1979 to 2005, municipal water-service areas have expanded, and the number of municipal water utilities rose from 472 to 611. The total amount of public-supply water has stabilized somewhat and may be declining from such factors as the

closing of large water-volume industries and implementation of water-conservation measures and leak-detection programs. In fact, public-supply delivery data provided in table 20 show that most change has occurred from a reduction of industrial delivery. In 1979, the industrial delivery was 173.6 Mgal/d and in 2005 it was 114.4 Mgal/d, combined with a decrease in public use and loss since 1990 of 66 Mgal/d. Domestic delivery has steadily increased since 1985 from 169.4 to 228.8 Mgal/d in 2005 along with a slight increase in commercial water deliveries from 92.2 Mgal/d in 1979 to 108.3 Mgal/d in 2005.

Self-supplied domestic per-capita use fluctuated throughout the compilation period (fig. 12d). It was not determined whether this is an artifact of the estimation method or if people are moving in and out of public-supply areas. For most water-use compilations, a per-capita-use value of 50 gal/d was applied. This value deviated in 2000 at of 55 gal/d and in 2005 when the value varied by county, although the State median per-capita-use value was 49 gal/d. Further comparisons of water withdrawals and per-capita water use for Wisconsin were summarized in a regional report covering 1950–1995 (Kay, 2002).

Table 19. Estimated total, public-supply, and domestic per-capita water use in Wisconsin, 1950–2005.

[Population reported in 1000s of persons; Mgal/d, million gallons per day; gal/d/person, per-capita use in gallons per day per person]

Year	State population	Total water use from select water-use categories (Mgal/d)	Total per-capita use from select water-use categories (gal/d/person)	Population served by public supply	Public-supply water use (Mgal/d)	Public-supply per-capita use (gal/d/person)	Self-supplied domestic population	Domestic water use (Mgal/d)	Domestic per-capita use (gal/d/person)
1950	3,434.58	479.47	140	2,232.47	290.00	130	1,202.10	60.00	50
1955	3,693.18	563.00	152	2,400.56	330.00	137	1,292.61	55.00	43
1960	3,951.78	758.30	192	2,568.66	370.00	144	1,383.12	70.00	51
1965	4,184.75	935.00	223	2,720.09	450.00	165	1,464.66	82.00	56
1970	4,417.73	1,018.00	230	2,871.53	490.00	171	1,546.21	74.00	48
1975	4,581.70	990.00	216	2,978.11	460.00	154	1,603.60	70.00	44
1979	4,705.64	1,224.90	260	3,104.12	564.00	182	1,601.65	72.88	46
1985	4,804.49	1,298.30	270	3,128.51	575.26	184	1,675.98	84.05	50
1990	4,891.76	1,345.10	275	3,405.94	595.32	175	1,485.83	90.15	61
1995	5,102.47	1,397.90	274	3,558.24	599.81	169	1,544.23	92.45	60
2000	5,363.71	1,482.30	276	3,616.17	623.15	172	1,747.53	96.28	55
2005	5,536.20	1,595.98	288	3,870.46	552.39	143	1,665.74	87.32	52[a]

[a]The 2005 State domestic per-capita value of 52 gal/d was calculated directly from these table data; however, community-level datasets analyzed by county provide a State average per capita of 50 gal/d/person.

Note: Totals do not necessarily equal the sum of parts or may not be comparable to other table totals because of rounding.

Table 20. Public-supply water use by water source and delivery type, excluding thermoelectric-power generation, in Wisconsin, 1950–2005.

[Withdrawals in million gallons per day; na, not analyzed; --, data not available]

Public-supply water use	1950	1955	1960	1965	1970	1975	1979	1985	1990	1995	2000	2005
By water source												
Ground water	120	140	160	180	220	190	289.00	274.64	294.24	311.22	329.76	305.42
Surface water	170	190	210	270	270	270	276.00	300.47	301.03	288.53	293.39	246.97
By water delivery												
Domestic	--	--	--	--	--	--	180.00	169.44	178.69	188.84	na	228.83
Commercial	--	--	--	--	--	--	92.00	97.84	98.80	111.33	na	108.30
Industrial	--	--	--	--	--	--	173.00	152.96	151.18	151.09	na	114.35
Public use and loss	--	--	--	--	--	--	120.00	154.87	166.60	148.49	na	100.91
Total	290	330	370	450	490	460	565.00	575.11	595.27	599.75	623.15	552.39

Note: Totals do not necessarily equal the sum of parts or may not be comparable to other table totals because of rounding.

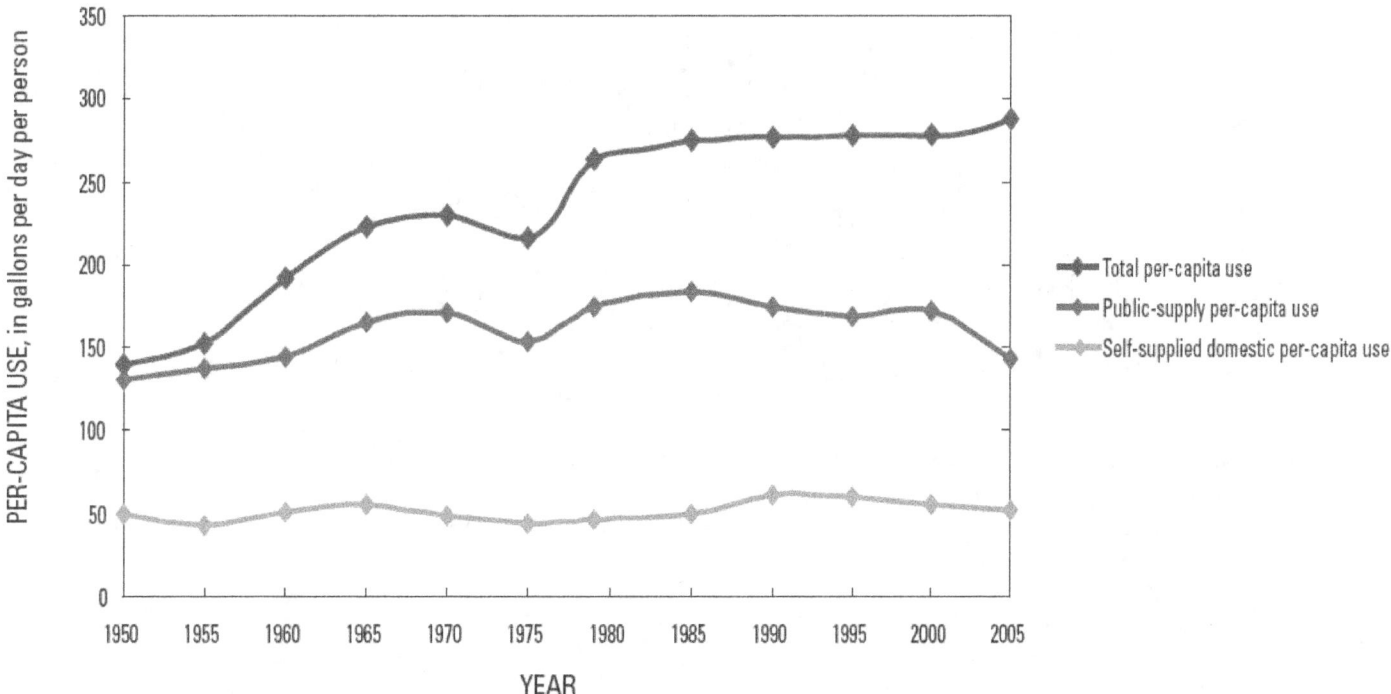

Figure 12a. Per-capita water use by total use, public-supply use, and domestic use in Wisconsin, 1950–2005 (Figure 12a corresponds with table 19.)

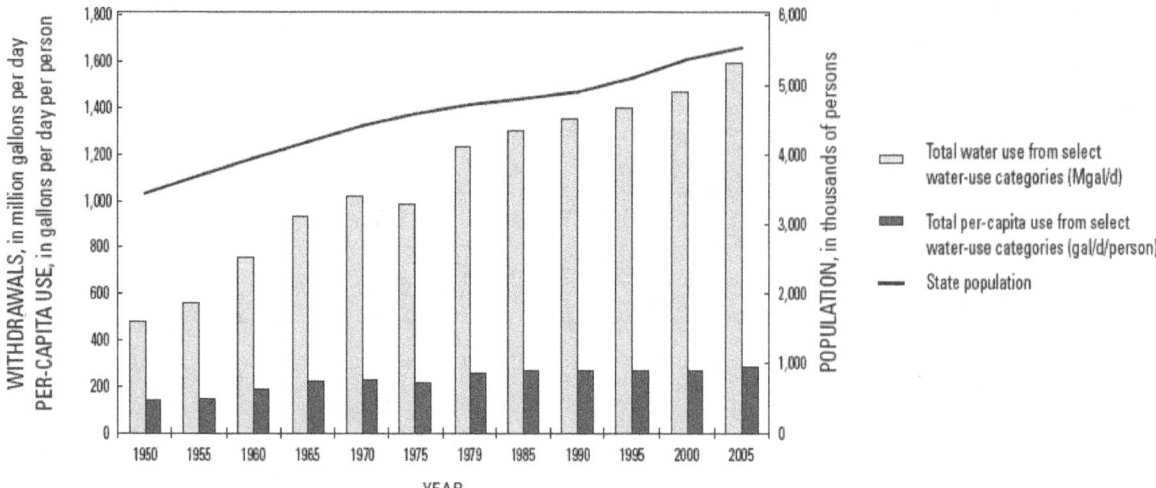

Figure 12b.   Total water use of select water-use categories and total per-capita water use in Wisconsin, 1950–2005. (Figure 12b corresponds with tables 18 and 19.)

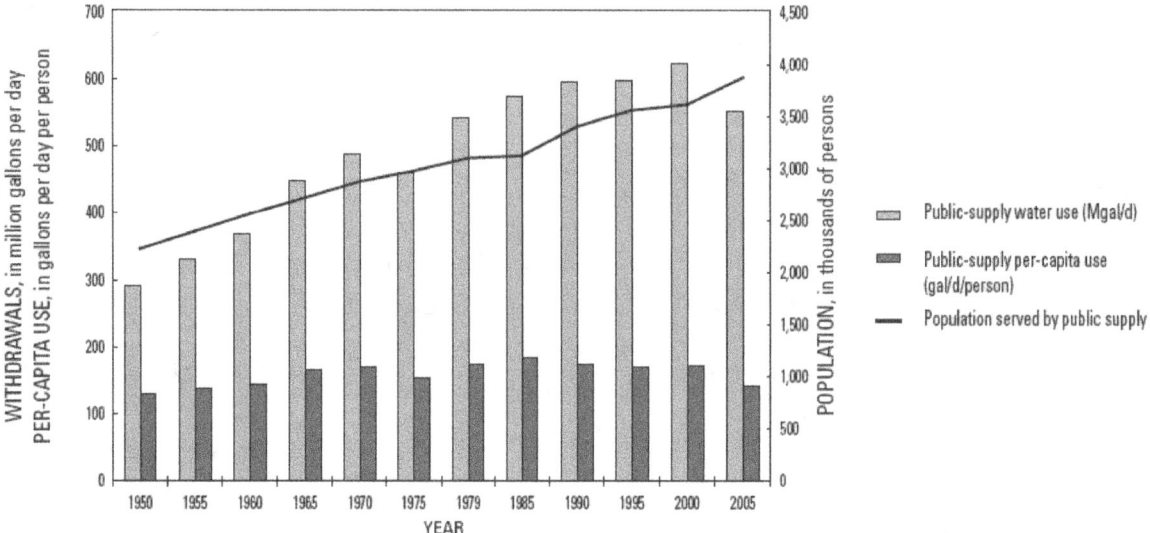

Figure 12c.   Public-supply water use and public-supply per-capita water use in Wisconsin, 1950–2005. (Figure 12c corresponds with tables 19 and 20.)

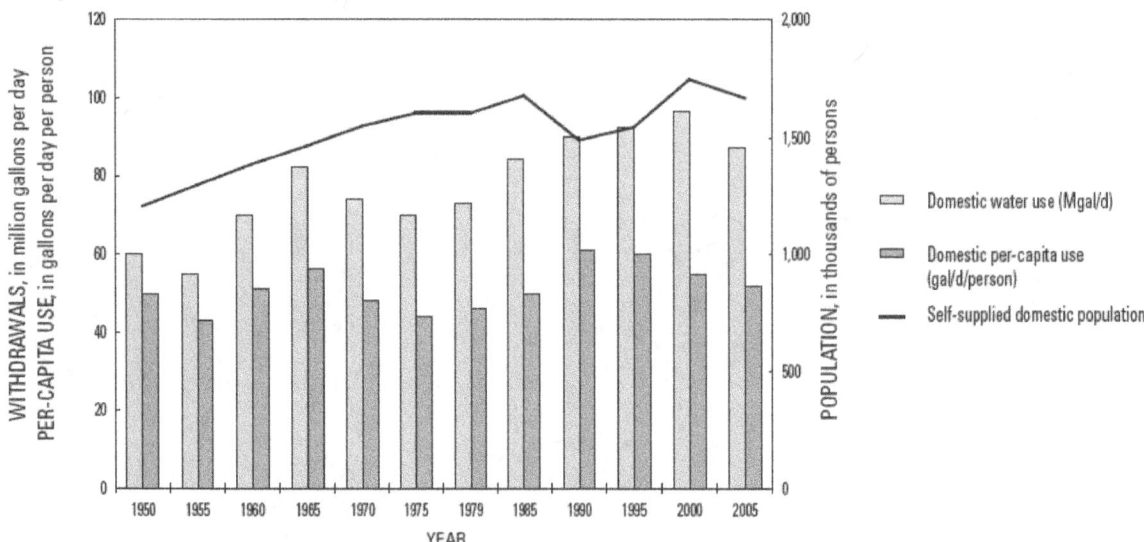

Figure 12d.   Domestic water use and domestic per-capita water use in Wisconsin, 1950–2005. (Figure 12d corresponds with table 19.)

Summary and Conclusions

The U.S. Geological (USGS) Wisconsin Water Science Center (WI WSC) estimated the quantity of surface and ground water used during 2005 in Wisconsin. Estimates also were made by county, subbasin (8-digit hydrologic unit code), and for eight water-use categories: public supply and self-supplied domestic; irrigation; non-irrigational agriculture (livestock and aquaculture); industrial; commercial; thermoelectric power; and mining. In-stream water uses, including hydroelectric-power generation, were not considered.

About 8,608 million gallons per day (Mgal/d) of water were withdrawn from surface- and ground-water sources in 2005, with about 7,622 Mgal/d (89 percent) from surface-water sources and about 986 Mgal/d (11 percent) from ground-water sources. The proportions of surface- and ground-water withdrawals were, for the most part, similar to those withdrawn for 2000. The largest surface-water withdrawals, including water used for thermoelectric-power generation, were in Manitowoc and Milwaukee Counties, about 2,135 and 1,219 Mgal/d, respectively. Excluding thermoelectric power, the two counties with the largest surface-water withdrawals were Milwaukee and Wood Counties, about 144 and 124 Mgal/d, respectively. The largest ground-water withdrawals were in Portage and Dane Counties, about 117 and 69.1 Mgal/d, respectively.

Total withdrawals for public supply were 552 Mgal/d of which 247 Mgal/d were from surface-water sources and 305 Mgal/d were from ground-water sources. Milwaukee County withdrew 137 Mgal/d of surface water from Lake Michigan, which was more surface water for public supply than any other county in the State. Dane County withdrew 50.1 Mgal/d, which was more ground water for public supply than any other county in the State. Estimates were made by summing available data from Public Service Commission of Wisconsin annual water-utility reports augmented with estimates based on information from the U.S. Environmental Protection Agency Safe Drinking Water Information System (SDWIS) database. Public-supply withdrawal for 2005 was 11 percent less than that of 2000.

The total self-supplied domestic-water withdrawal for 2005 was estimated at 87.3 Mgal/d of which 100 percent was assumed to be from ground-water sources. Estimates were made by multiplying domestic self-supplied population by a domestic self-supplied per-capita use coefficient for each county. Domestic withdrawal for 2005 was about 9 percent less than the estimate for 2000.

About 402 Mgal/d of water were withdrawn for self-supplied irrigation from surface- and ground-water sources in 2005, with about 15.2 Mgal/d from surface-water sources and about 387 Mgal/d from ground-water sources. These estimates included water use for agriculture and golf courses along with a newly added subcategory for other irrigation. Agricultural-irrigation estimates were based on a water-application rate per irrigated acre and golf course estimates were made based on a water application per number of holes. Other irrigation was identified from Wisconsin Department of Natural Resources (WDNR) surface-water withdrawal permits and ground-water-well data sources; the estimation methods varied. Irrigation withdrawals for 2005 were 78 percent greater than those in 2000, although the reported 2005 estimate is believed to be at the high end of the range for irrigation water use.

Water withdrawals for self-supplied non-irrigational agricultural use were estimated for aquaculture at 43.2 Mgal/d from surface-water sources and about 38.5 Mgal/d from ground-water sources. Water withdrawals for livestock were estimated at 7.27 Mgal/d from surface-water sources and about 65.6 Mgal/d from ground-water sources. The estimates for aquaculture were made by combining past reported water-use data, recent data from inquiry responses, and a default water-use value for facilities without associated water-use data. The estimates for livestock were based on applying an animal-specific water-requirement coefficient to National Agricultural Statistics Service (NASS) Census data for livestock counts. Aquacultural withdrawals for 2005 included additional private facilities and were estimated at about 16 percent greater than those in 2000. Livestock coefficients were updated for 2005 and were about 10 percent greater than those in 2000.

Water withdrawal by self-supplied industries was about 471 Mgal/d in 2005. It is estimated that 400 Mgal/d were from surface-water sources, mostly by lumber, pulp, and paper industries for processing and cooling (about 86 percent or 344 Mgal/d), and about 70.9 Mgal/d were from ground-water sources. Estimates were made by compiling a site inventory and either assigning past reported water-use data or applying water-use coefficients for the type of industrial facility (defined by the Standard Industrial Classification (SIC) code categories) or water-use purpose. Self-supplied industrial withdrawals increased about 4 percent from 451 Mgal/d in 2000.

Water withdrawal for self-supplied commercial use was about 10.7 Mgal/d in 2005. All self-supplied commercial water use was assumed to be from ground-water sources. There were no self-supplied commercial data collected in 2000. Estimates were made by the same methods applied in the self-supplied industrial category. Estimated commercial withdrawals for 2005 were about 32 percent less than those in 1995.

There were 30 fossil-fuel, steam-generating thermoelectric-power plants and non-utility facilities (predominantly industries) that operated in 2005. Most plants and facilities have once-through cooling systems. Water withdrawal from surface-water sources was about 6,895 Mgal/d. Water withdrawal from ground-water sources was minimal, about 3.37 Mgal/d for a plant identified with a recirculation cooling system and for other power-plant or facility uses, such as water used for fly-ash control or other plant-cooling requirements. Thermoelectric power used the greatest amount of water compared to the other water-use categories. Most of the information on total withdrawals and energy produced for this category was from U.S.

Department of Energy (DOE) and Public Service Commission of Wisconsin (PSC) sources; however, estimates for power at private industrial facilities were based on power-plant capacity data. Withdrawals for thermoelectric power in 2005 were about 13 percent greater than those in 2000, which is largely owing to the identification of additional pulp and paper industries.

Water withdrawal for self-supplied mining was about 14.9 Mgal/d from surface-water sources and about 17.6 Mgal/d from ground-water sources. There were no mining data collected in 2000; in 2005 these data were provided by the National Water-Use Information Program. Mining withdrawals in 2005 were about 246 and 122 percent greater for surface- and ground-water, respectively, than those in 1995.

It is possible for estimation methods or objectives applied in 2005 to have changed since the last water-use estimation year (2000), referred to in this report as a compilation, or throughout previous compilations (1950–1995). Such updates may have an affect on apparent trends. In general, changes occur in the availability of data and information about water use, data sources and estimation methods, or the inclusion and exclusion of certain water-use categories. The largest differences applied in the 2005 compilation (since the 2000 compilation) were the following: (1) a county rather than State per-capita-use value was applied as the coefficient for self-supplied domestic water use; (2) the estimation method for crop irrigation changed; (3) the industrial well inventory was updated; (4) self-supplied commercial and mining water uses were reinstated; and (5) the thermoelectric water-use category now includes estimates for water withdrawn and electricity generated at additional facilities not previously identified, especially privately owned industrial facilities. Other minor differences do exist, and those that are notable include the following: (1) the irrigation water-use category includes an estimate for other irrigation (not for crop or golf course purposes); (2) the golf course estimation method was slightly revised to allow for uncertainty at facilities that may not irrigate or may receive public-supply water; (3) livestock water-use coefficients were slightly modified; and (4) a more complete inventory of private aquacultural facilities was possible, and new water-use defaults were created for facilities with no available water-use information.

At 5-year intervals, the USGS WI WSC provides water-use data from Wisconsin for the national reports, "Estimated Use of Water in the United States," which are available (back to 1950) at http://water.usgs.gov/watuse/50years html. For additional information and data or to learn more about water use specific to Wisconsin, refer to the USGS WI WSC website at http://wi.water.usgs.gov/water-use/.

Acknowledgments

This study was made possible by the assistance of many people who helped in the compilation, provided information and data, and reviewed this report. The author is very grateful to T. Adam Gallagher, Elizabeth Woodcock, Ryan Carr, and Austin Baldwin for their considerable help with the data and information assembled for this project. The author thanks John Marks of the Wisconsin Department of Agriculture, Trade and Consumer Protection for providing livestock water-use explanations and animal per-capita use coefficients. Laura Churn, Jeff Helmuth, Bill Furbish, Shaili Pfeiffer, and Mary Vollbrecht of the Wisconsin Department of Natural Resources are thanked for exchanging information and for sharing details about their water approval and permitting programs. Appreciation is extended to Kate West and Bob Biebel of the Southeastern Wisconsin Regional Planning Commission and Bruce Schmidt and Jeff Ripp of the Public Service Commission of Wisconsin–Water Division for their time spent in providing water-use data and replies. Scot Cullen and Jim Lepinski of the Public Service Commission of Wisconsin–Energy Division are thanked for providing additional power-plant data and information. Madeline Gotkowitz of the University of Wisconsin–Extension Wisconsin Geological and Natural History Survey is thanked for disclosing her findings on agricultural irrigation water-application rates prior to publication. Tom Schwab of the O.J. Noer Turf Grass Research & Education Facility is thanked for his assistance with estimating golf course irrigation, and David Fischer of the University of Wisconsin–Extension Agriculture and Natural Resources is thanked for providing further detailed information about crop irrigation in Wisconsin. The author is very grateful to several aquacultural facilities that provided detailed information about water use in their operations. Larry Lynch (WDNR) and Carol Luukonnen (USGS) are thanked for providing valuable technical-review comments as well as Bonnie Stich Fink, Greg Tracy, and Charles Dunning for additional editorial review, which has improved this report.

Selected References

Bajwa, R.S., Crosswhite, W.M., Hostetler, J.E., and Wright, O.W., 1992, Agricultural irrigation and water use: Rockville, Md., U.S. Department of Agriculture, Resources and Technology Division, Economic Research Service, Agriculture Information Bulletin 638, Jan. 1992, 116 p.

Dawson, Tom, 2003, Wisconsin law of groundwater withdrawal—A primer, in 2003 Wisconsin Lakes Convention, Green Bay, Wis., April 10–12, 2003, Proceedings: Madison, Wis., Wisconsin Department of Natural Resources–Wisconsin Groundwater Coordinating Council, Breakout Session A—Water supply—Will there be enough and why is getting enough becoming more and more difficult?, accessed January 8, 2009, at http://www.dnr.state.wi.us/org/water/dwg/gcc/TD-TalkOutline.pdf

Ellefson, B.R., Fan, C.H., and Ripley, J.L., 1997, Water use in Wisconsin, 1995: U.S. Geological Survey Open-File Report 97–356, 1 sheet.

Ellefson, B.R., Mueller, G.D., and Buchwald, C.A., 2002, Water use in Wisconsin, 2000: U.S. Geological Survey Open-File Report 02–356, 1 sheet.

Ellefson, B.R., Rury, K.S., Krohelski, J.T., 1987, Water use in Wisconsin, 1985: U.S. Geological Survey Open-File Report 87–699, 1 sheet.

Ellefson, B.R., Sabin, T.J., Krohelski, J.T., 1993, Water use in Wisconsin, 1990: U.S. Geological Survey Open-File Report 93–118, 1 sheet.

Energy and Environmental Analysis, Inc., 2007, Combined heat and power units located in Wisconsin, accessed August 28, 2006, at http://www.eea-inc.com/chpdata/States/WI html

Environmental Working Group, 2005, National tap water quality database—A national assessment of tap water quality, accessed January 9, 2009, at http://www.ewg.org/tapwater/findings.php

GolfLink, 2009, Golf course directory, accessed January 9, 2009, at http://www.golflink.com/golf-courses/course-directory.aspx

GolfWisconsin, 2009, Wisconsin golf course guide, accessed January 9, 2009, at http://wisconsingolfonline.com/directory/index.cfm

Gotkowitz, M., Hart, D., and Dunning, C., 2008, Groundwater sustainability in a humid climate—Groundwater pumping, groundwater consumption, and land-use change: Wisconsin Geologic and Natural History Survey, Open-File Report 2008–2, 47 p., 16 color pl. [Also on CD–Rom in PDF format].

Hanson, A.C., 2002, Brewing land use conflicts—Wisconsin's Right to Farm Law: Wisconsin Lawyer, v. 75, no. 12, Dec. 2002, accessed January 12, 2009, at http://www.wisbar.org/AM/Template.cfm?Section=Wisconsin_Lawyer&template=/CM/ContentDisplay.cfm&contentid=53190#author

Hutson, S.S., compiler, 2007, Guidelines for preparation of State water-use estimates for 2005: U.S. Geological Survey Techniques and Methods Book 4, Chap. E1, 36 p., accessed January 9, 2009, at http://pubs.usgs.gov/tm/2007/tm4e1/

Hutson, S.S., Barber, N.L., Kenny, J.F., Linsey, K.S., Lumia, D.S., and Maupin, M.A., 2004, Estimated use of water in the United States in 2000: Reston, Va., U.S. Geological Survey Circular 1268, 46 p., accessed January 9, 2009, at http://pubs.usgs.gov/circ/2004/circ1268/

Kay, R.T., 2002, Estimated water withdrawals, water use, and water consumption in Illinois, Indiana, Iowa, Kentucky, Michigan, Missouri, and Wisconsin, 1950–95: U.S. Geological Survey Water-Resources Investigations Report 01–4116, 29 p.

Kenny, J.F. (editor), 2004, Guidelines for preparation of State water-use estimates for 2000: U.S. Geological Survey Techniques and Methods Report 4-A4, 49 p., at http://water.usgs.gov/watuse/

Krohelski, J.T., Ellefson, B.R., and Storlie, C.A., 1987, Estimated use of ground water for irrigation in Wisconsin, 1984: U.S. Geological Survey Water-Resources Investigations Report 86–4079, 12 p.

Lawrence, C.L., and Ellefson, B.R., 1982, Water use in Wisconsin, 1979: U.S. Geological Survey Water-Resources Investigations Report 82–444, 98 p.

Lawrence, C.L., Ellefson, B.R., and Cotter, R.D., 1984, Public-supply pumpage in Wisconsin, by aquifer: U.S. Geological Survey Open-File Report 83–931, 40 p.

Linn, James G., 1997, Nutritional management of lactating dairy cows during periods of heat stress: St. Paul, Minn., University of Minnesota-Extension Dairy Update, Issue 125, February 1997, accessed February 9, 2009, at http://www.ansci.umn.edu/dairy/dairyupdates/du125 htm

MacKichan, K.A., 1951, Estimated use of water in the United States—1950: U.S. Geological Survey Circular 115, 13 p.

MacKichan, K.A., 1957, Estimated use of water in the United States, 1955: U.S. Geological Survey Circular 398, 18 p.

Marella, R.L., 2004, Water withdrawals, use, discharge, and trends in Florida, 2000: U.S. Geological Survey Scientific Investigations Report 2004-5151, 136 p.

MacKichan, K.A., and Kammerer, J.C., 1961, Estimated use of water in the United States, 1960: U.S. Geological Survey Circular 456, 26 p.

Minnesota Department of Natural Resources, 2007, Water use—Water Appropriations Permit Program, accessed June 26, 2007, at http://www.dnr.state.mn.us/waters/watermgmt_section/appropriations/wateruse html

Multi-Resolution Land Characteristics Consortium, 2001, National Land Cover Database 2001, accessed January 12, 2009, at http://www mrlc.gov/

Murray, C.R., 1968, Estimated use of water in the United States, 1965: U.S. Geological Survey Circular 556, 53 p.

Murray, C.R., and Reeves, E.B., 1972, Estimated use of water in the United States in 1970: U.S. Geological Survey Circular 676, 37 p.

Murray, C.R., and Reeves, E.B., 1977, Estimated use of water in the United States in 1975: U.S. Geological Survey Circular 765, 39 p.

National Research Council, 2002, Estimating water use in the United States—A new paradigm for the National Water-Use Information Program: Washington D.C., National Academy Press, 176 p.

Olcott, P.G., 1992, Ground water atlas of the United States—Iowa, Michigan, Minnesota, Wisconsin: U.S. Geological Survey Hydrologic Atlas 730–J, 31 p.

Pira, Edward, 1997, A guide to golf course irrigation system design and drainage: Chelsea, Mich., Ann Arbor Press, 434 p.

Public Service Commission of Wisconsin, 2005, Municipal annual report data, accessed January 12, 2009, at http://psc.wi.gov/apps/wegs/content/criteria.asp?type=water

Schmid, A.A., 1961, Water allocation by permit in Wisconsin: Land Economics, v. 37, no. 2, p. 182–187.

Solley, W.B., Chase, E.B., and Mann, W.B., IV, 1983, Estimated use of water in the United States in 1980: U.S. Geological Survey Circular 1001, 56 p.

Solley, W.B., Merk, C.F., and Pierce, R.R., 1988, Estimated use of water in the United States in 1985: U.S. Geological Survey Circular 1004, 82 p.

Solley, W.B., Pierce, R.R., and Perlman, H.A., 1993, Estimated use of water in the United States in 1990: U.S. Geological Survey Circular 1081, 76 p.

Solley, W.B., Pierce, R.R., and Perlman, H.A., 1998, Estimated use of water in the United States in 1995: U.S. Geological Survey Circular 1200, 71 p.

Sun, R.J., Weeks, J.B., and Grubb, H.F., 1997, Bibliography of Regional Aquifer-Systems Analysis Program of the U.S. Geological Survey, 1978–96: U.S. Geological Survey Water-Resources Investigations Report 97–4074, 63 p., accessed January 9, 2009, at http://water.usgs.gov/ogw/rasa/html/introduction html

U.S. Census Bureau, 2003, Census 2000—Census of population and housing, accessed January 12, 2009, at http://factfinder.census.gov/servlet/DatasetMainPageServlet?_program=DEC&_submenuId=&_lang=en&_ts

U.S. Census Bureau, 2006, County population datasets—Population data by county for 2005, accessed March 21, 2006, at http://www.census.gov/popest/datasets html

U.S. Census Bureau, 1995, Wisconsin—Population of counties by decennial census—1900 to 1990, accessed May 22, 2009, at http://www.census.gov/population/cencounts/wi190090.txt

U.S. Department of Agriculture, 2004, Federal standards for delineation of hydrologic unit boundaries: National Cartography and Geospatial Center, v 2.0, October 1, 2004, 60 p., accessed January 12, 2009, at ftp://ftp-fc.sc.egov.usda.gov/NCGC/products/watershed/hu-standards.pdf

U.S. Department of Agriculture–National Agricultural Statistics Service, 1994, 1992 Census of agriculture, volume 1, part 49, chapter 1, Wisconsin State and County data, State data—Table 1, Historical highlights—1992 and earlier census years, accessed January 12, 2009, at http://www.agcensus.usda.gov/Publications/1992/Volume_1/Wisconsin/wi1_01.pdf

U.S. Department of Agriculture–National Agricultural Statistics Service, 1999, 1997 Census of agriculture—Ranking of States and counties: AC97–S–2, v. 2, subject ser. pt. 2, 110 p., accessed January 12, 2009, at http://www.agcensus.usda.gov/Publications/1997/Rankings_of_State_and_Counties/ac97s-3r.pdf

U.S. Department of Agriculture–National Agricultural Statistics Service, 2004a, 2004 Wisconsin agricultural statistics, accessed December 6, 2004, at http://www nass.usda.gov/wi

U.S. Department of Agriculture–National Agricultural Statistics Service, 2004b, 2002 Census of agriculture—Wisconsin State and County data: AC-02-A-49, v. 1, geographic area ser. pt. 49 [variously paged], accessed January 12, 2009, at http://www.agcensus.usda.gov/Publications/2002/Volume_1,_Chapter_1_State_Level/Wisconsin/WIVolume104

U.S. Department of Agriculture–National Agricultural Statistics Service, 2004c, 2002 Census of agriculture—2003 farm and ranch irrigation survey: AC-02-SS-1, v. 3, special studies pt. 1, 193 p.

U.S. Department of Agriculture–National Agricultural Statistics Service, 2006, 2002 Census of agriculture—2005 Census of aquaculture—Table 5–Sources of water used for aquaculture production, by State and United States—2005 and 1998, accessed January 8, 2009, at http://www.agcensus.usda.gov/Publications/2002/Aquaculture/aquacen2005_05.pdf

U.S. Department of Agriculture–Natural Resources Conservation Service, 2008, Watershed boundary dataset (WBD), accessed January 12, 2009, at http://www ncgc.nrcs.usda.gov/products/datasets/watershed/

U.S. Department of Energy–Energy Information Administration, 2004a, Annual steam-electric plant operation and design data, accessed June 26, 2006, at http://www.eia.doe.gov/cneaf/electricity/page/eia767 html

U.S. Department of Energy–Energy Information Administration, 2004b, Monthly utility power plant database, accessed June 26, 2006, at http://www.eia.doe.gov/cneaf/electricity/page/eia906u.html

U.S. Environmental Protection Agency, 1995, Water trivia facts: Office of Water 4601, EPA 810–F–95–001, April 1995, accessed January 12, 2009, at http://media mgbg.com/wkrg/photos/weather/downloads/Water_Facts.pdf

U.S. Environmental Protection Agency, 2006, Safe Drinking Water Information System (SDWIS), accessed March 23, 2007, at http://oaspub.epa.gov/enviro/sdw_form_v2.create_page?state_abbr=WI

U.S. Geological Survey, 2008a, National handbook of recommended methods for water data acquisition—Chapter 11—Water use, accessed January 9, 2009, at http://pubs.usgs.gov/chapter11/

U.S. Geological Survey, 2008b, National Water Information System—Web interface, accessed January 9, 2009, at http://waterdata.usgs.gov/nwis

U.S. Geological Survey, 2008c, Wisconsin water-use data, accessed January 9, 2009, at http://wi.water.usgs.gov/data/wateruse html

U.S. Geological Survey, 2008d, Estimated use of water in the United States in 2000—Glossary, accessed January 9, 2009, at http://pubs.usgs.gov/circ/2004/circ1268/htdocs/text-glossary html

U.S. Golf Course Finder, 2008, Wisconsin golf courses, accessed January 12, 2009, at http://search.golf.com/golf-courses/us/WI html

Wisconsin Department of Administration–Demographic Services Center, 2006, Table—Time series of the final official population estimates and census counts for Wisconsin municipalities in existence on January 1, 2006, accessed March 1, 2007, at http://www.doa.state.wi.us/subcategory.asp?linksubcatid=96&linkcatid=11&linkid=64&locid=9

Wisconsin Department of Agriculture, Trade and Consumer Protection, 1998, 1998 Wisconsin aquaculture directory: Madison, Wis., Division of Marketing, Agricultural Development and Diversification, 74p.

Wisconsin Department of Natural Resources, 1997, Status of groundwater quantity in Wisconsin: PUBL-DG-043-97, April 1997, accessed January 12, 2009, at http://www.dnr.state.wi.us/org/water/dwg/gcc/gw-quantity.pdf

Wisconsin Department of Natural Resources, 1998, GEODISC 3.0—A geographic information datasharing CD–ROM: Madison, Wis., Bureau of Enterprise Information Technology and Applications, Geographic Services Section, [rev. October 22, 1998], accessed January 12, 2009, at ftp://dnrftp01.wi.gov/geodata/

Wisconsin Department of Natural Resources, 2004, Mining in Wisconsin, accessed July 24, 2004, at http://www.dnr.state.wi.us/org/aw/wm/mining/

Wisconsin Department of Natural Resources, 2005a, Groundwater retrieval network and high capacity well database: Bureau of Drinking Water and Groundwater, accessed December 7, 2005, at http://dnr.wi.gov/org/water/dwg/index.htm

Wisconsin Department of Natural Resources, 2005b, High-capacity well terms and definitions, accessed March 3, 2005, at http://dnr.wi.gov/org/water/dwg/hicap.html

Wisconsin Department of Natural Resources, 2007, Bureau of Drinking Water and Groundwater, water well data, ver. 3: CD–ROM, July 2007.

Wisconsin Department of Natural Resources, 2008a, DNR regions, accessed May 11, 2008, at http://sotw.dnr.state.wi.us/sotw/RegionPop.do

Wisconsin Department of Natural Resources, 2008b, Wisconsin lakes facts, accessed August 19, 2008, at http://dnr.wi.gov/org/water/division/yow/lakes htm

Wisconsin Department of Natural Resources, 2008c, Wisconsin rivers facts, accessed August 19, 2008, at http://dnr.wi.gov/org/water/division/yow/rivers htm

Wisconsin Groundwater Coordinating Council, 2007, Report to the Legislature—Groundwater—Wisconsin's buried treasure, accessed January 12, 2009, at http://www.dnr.state.wi.us/org/water/dwg/gcc/rtl/2007report.pdf

Wisconsin Office of the Governor, 2005, Relating to a proclamation declaring a State of emergency relating to drought conditions: Executive Order No. 111, 15 July 2005, 2 p., accessed January 12, 2009, at http://www.wisgov.state.wi.us/docview.asp?docid=3383&locid=19

Wisconsin State Legislature, 2000, Chapter NR 142—Wisconsin water management and conservation: Register, March 2000, no. 531, p. 351–355, accessed January 12, 2009, at http://www.legis.state.wi.us/rsb/code/nr/nr142.pdf

Wisconsin State Legislature, 2004, 2003 Wisconsin Act 310—Regulation of high capacity wells, notification of well construction, groundwater quantity management, granting rule-making authority, and making appropriations: Wisconsin Law Archive, 2003 Assembly Bill 926, 6 p., accessed January 12, 2009, at http://www.legis.state.wi.us/2003/data/acts/03Act310.pdf

Wisconsin State Legislature, 2006, Chapter NR 812—Well construction and pump installation: Register, January 2006, no. 601, p. 123–225, accessed January 12, 2009, at http://www.legis.state.wi.us/rsb/code/nr/nr812.pdf

Wisconsin State Legislature, 2007, Chapter NR 820—Groundwater quantity protection: Register, August 2007, no. 620, p. 233–237, accessed January 12, 2009, at http://www.legis.state.wi.us/rsb/code/nr/nr820.pdf

Appendixes

Appendix 1a. Population Estimates, Area, and Population Density of Wisconsin, by County, 2005

[Data sources: population from U.S. Census Bureau (2006); land area from Wisconsin Department of Natural Resources (1998); land type from Multi-Resolution Land Characteristics Consortium (2001); population, in persons; area, in mi^2, square miles]

County	2000 census population	2005 estimated population	Total area (mi^2)	Water area[a] (mi^2)	Land area (mi^2)	2005 population density[b] (persons/mi^2)
Adams	18,643	20,828	688	103	585	36
Ashland	16,866	16,627	1,053	250	803	21
Barron	44,963	45,834	890	68	821	56
Bayfield	15,013	15,145	1,510	105	1,405	11
Brown	226,778	238,987	534	35	500	478
Buffalo	13,804	13,968	709	77	632	22
Burnett	15,674	16,528	880	173	707	23
Calumet	40,631	44,137	397	104	293	151
Chippewa	55,195	59,950	1,041	117	923	65
Clark	33,557	34,098	1,218	46	1,172	29
Columbia	52,468	55,364	795	112	683	81
Crawford	17,243	17,134	599	64	535	32
Dane	426,526	458,106	1,237	92	1,146	400
Dodge	85,897	88,103	907	148	758	116
Door	27,961	28,349	487	106	381	74
Douglas	43,287	44,208	1,338	245	1,093	40
Dunn	39,858	41,708	864	64	800	52
Eau Claire	93,142	94,089	645	42	603	156
Florence	5,088	4,974	497	107	390	13
Fond du Lac	97,296	99,337	765	127	639	156
Forest	10,024	9,961	1,046	322	724	14
Grant	49,597	49,671	1180	60	1,119	44
Green	33,647	35,165	584	13	571	62
Green Lake	19,105	19,168	380	93	287	67
Iowa	22,780	23,569	767	25	743	32
Iron	6,861	6,649	802	281	521	13
Jackson	19,100	19,758	999	107	892	22
Jefferson	74,021	79,328	582	117	465	171
Juneau	24,316	26,725	803	161	642	42
Kenosha	149,577	160,544	279	13	266	604
Kewaunee	20,187	20,840	344	51	293	71
La Crosse	107,120	108,958	480	58	422	258
Lafayette	16,137	16,310	634	5	629	26
Langlade	20,740	20,735	887	178	709	29
Lincoln	29,641	30,319	906	220	687	44
Manitowoc	82,887	81,949	595	81	514	159
Marathon	125,834	128,941	1,575	155	1,420	91
Marinette	43,384	43,406	1,429	329	1,100	39
Marquette	15,832	15,237	464	100	364	42

Appendix 1a. Population Estimates, Area, and Population Density of Wisconsin, by County, 2005—Continued.

[Data sources: population from U.S. Census Bureau (2006); land area from Wisconsin Department of Natural Resources (1998); land type from Multi-Resolution Land Characteristics Consortium (2001); population, in persons; area, in mi², square miles]

County	2000 census population	2005 estimated population	Total area (mi²)	Water area[a] (mi²)	Land area (mi²)	2005 population density[b] (persons/mi²)
Menominee	4,562	4,580	365	110	255	18
Milwaukee	940,164	921,654	242	8	235	3,926
Monroe	40,899	42,644	908	41	866	49
Oconto	35,634	37,666	1,017	202	815	46
Oneida	36,776	36,994	1,235	522	713	52
Outagamie	160,971	171,006	644	74	570	300
Ozaukee	82,317	86,072	234	23	211	408
Pepin	7,213	7,380	249	30	219	34
Pierce	36,804	39,102	591	25	567	69
Polk	41,319	44,329	956	77	879	50
Portage	67,182	67,585	822	77	745	91
Price	15,822	15,220	1,277	420	858	18
Racine	188,831	195,708	340	16	324	604
Richland	17,924	18,403	589	14	575	32
Rock	152,307	157,538	726	29	697	226
Rusk	15,347	15,198	930	177	754	20
St. Croix	63,155	77,144	848	25	823	94
Sauk	55,225	57,746	1,349	44	1,305	44
Sawyer	16,196	16,975	909	294	615	28
Shawano	40,664	41,335	517	191	326	127
Sheboygan	112,646	114,610	736	52	684	168
Taylor	19,680	19,766	984	156	828	24
Trempealeau	27,010	27,812	742	33	708	39
Vernon	28,056	29,055	816	31	785	37
Vilas	21,033	22,330	1,017	384	633	35
Walworth	93,759	99,844	576	37	539	185
Washburn	16,036	16,601	853	131	722	23
Washington	117,493	126,158	436	50	386	327
Waukesha	360,767	378,971	580	77	504	752
Waupaca	51,731	52,563	765	121	643	82
Waushara	23,154	24,789	637	80	557	44
Winnebago	156,763	159,482	578	193	386	414
Wood	75,555	75,234	809	138	671	112
Wisconsin	5,363,675	5,536,201	56,069	8,435	47,634	

[a] Water area defined for this report to include open water and wetlands.

[b] Population density is based on land area and not total area.

Appendix 1b. Population Estimates, Area, and Population Density of Wisconsin, by Subbasin, 2005

[Data sources: population from U.S. Census Bureau (2006); land area from Wisconsin Department of Natural Resources (1998); land type from Multi-Resolution Land Characteristics Consortium (2001); population, in persons; area, in mi², square miles; na, not applicable]

Subbasin 8-digit hydrologic unit code	Hydrologic unit name (Subbasin name)	2005 estimated population	Total area (mi²)	Water area (mi²)	Land area (mi²)	2005 population density[b], (persons/mi²)
04010201	St. Louis River[a]	19,980	76	12	64	313
04010301	Beartrap-Nemadji Rivers	40,521	1,647	140	1,508	27
04010302	Bad-Montreal Rivers	11,425	1,202	186	1,016	11
04020101	Black-Presque Isle Rivers[a]	0	76	29	47	0
04020102	Ontonagon River[a]	0	40	17	23	0
04020300	Lake Superior	na	na	na	na	na
04030101	Manitowoc-Sheboygan Rivers	243,540	1,629	193	1,436	170
04030102	Door-Kewaunee Rivers	56,888	765	145	620	92
04030103	Pensaukee River	15,890	333	34	299	53
04030104	Oconto River	31,386	960	206	755	42
04030105	Peshtigo River	35,373	1,219	282	937	38
04030106	Brule River	2,042	185	44	141	14
04030108	Menominee River	17,310	1,346	354	992	17
04030201	Upper Fox River	136,991	1,619	305	1,315	104
04030202	Wolf River	162,604	3,724	747	2,977	55
04030203	Lake Winnebago	82,220	572	246	326	252
04030204	Lower Fox River	420,220	647	30	617	681
04040002	Pike-Root Rivers	436,729	334	9	325	1,343
04040003	Milwaukee River	993,940	878	89	790	1,259
04060200	Lake Michigan	na	na	na	na	na
07030001	Upper St. Croix River	23,526	1,482	245	1,236	19
07030002	Namekagon River	14,682	1,018	179	839	17
07030005	Lower St. Croix River	131,886	1,701	155	1,546	85
07040001	Rush-Vermillion Rivers	25,076	513	37	476	53
07040003	Buffalo-Whitewater Rivers	22,435	737	70	667	34
07040005	Trempealeau River	18,612	729	19	710	26
07040006	La Crosse-Pine Rivers	119,045	600	51	549	217
07040007	Black River	64,007	2,274	181	2,093	31
07050001	Upper Chippewa River	13,379	1,931	483	1,448	9
07050002	Flambeau River	21,697	1,177	469	707	31
07050003	South Fork Flambeau River	8,248	739	295	443	19
07050004	Jump River	8,762	854	186	668	13
07050005	Lower Chippewa River	134,418	2,059	206	1,853	73
07050006	Eau Claire River	44,561	883	52	831	54
07050007	Red Cedar River	88,930	1,890	144	1,746	51
07060001	Coon-Yellow Rivers	30,316	674	76	598	51

Appendix 1b. Population Estimates, Area, and Population Density of Wisconsin, by Subbasin, 2005—Continued.

[Data sources: population from U.S. Census Bureau (2006); land area from Wisconsin Department of Natural Resources (1998); land type from Multi-Resolution Land Characteristics Consortium (2001); population, in persons; area, in mi², square miles; na, not applicable]

Subbasin 8-digit hydrologic unit code	Hydrologic unit name (Subbasin name)	2005 estimated population	Total area (mi²)	Water area (mi²)	Land area (mi²)	2005 population density[b], (persons/mi²)
07060003	Grant-Little Maquoketa Rivers	34,009	790	39	751	45
07060005	Apple-Plum Rivers	10,414	232	2	231	45
07070001	Upper Wisconsin River	63,909	2,136	827	1,309	49
07070002	Lake Dubay	166,490	2,717	366	2,351	71
07070003	Castle-Rock	203,284	3,247	532	2,715	75
07070004	Baraboo River	44,451	655	22	633	70
07070005	Lower Wisconsin River	100,936	2,360	145	2,215	46
07070006	Kickapoo River	22,307	767	10	757	29
07090001	Upper Rock River	230,230	1,892	268	1,624	142
07090002	Lower Rock River	661,390	1,819	192	1,627	406
07090003	Pecatonica River	46,032	1,143	9	1,134	41
07090004	Sugar River	82,070	691	23	669	123
07090005	Lower Rock-Piscasaw Creek[a]	1,354	14	0	14	98
07090006	Kishwaukee River[a]	4,025	31	0	31	129
07120004	Des Plaines River	21,882	135	5	130	169
07120006	Upper Fox River	366,799	926	79	847	433
Total		5,536,221	56,069	8,435	47,634	

[a] The majority of this subbasin is outside Wisconsin.

[b] Population density is based on land area and not total area.

Appendix 2. Overall water use by category and by subbasin in Wisconsin, 2005.

[Mgal/d, million gallons per day; gWh, gigawatthour(s) of energy produced; thermoelectric, thermoelectric power generation]

| | WITHDRAWALS, in Mgal/d | | | | | | | | | |
| | Public supply | | Domestic | | Irrigation | | Livestock | | Aquaculture | |
Subbasin 8-digit hydrologic unit code	Ground water	Surface water	Ground water	Surface water	Ground water	Surface water	Ground water	Surface water	Ground water	Surface water
04010201	0.01	0.00	0.04	0.00	0.02	0.00	0.01	0.00	0.00	0.00
04010301	.37	.00	.69	.00	.30	.02	.18	.02	3.91	.00
04010302	.27	.00	.28	.00	.17	.13	.11	.01	.00	.00
04020101	.00	.00	.00	.00	.08	.00	.00	.00	.00	.00
04020102	.00	.00	.00	.00	.05	.00	.00	.00	.00	.00
04020300	.00	4.01	.00	.00	.00	.00	.00	.00	.00	11.67
04030101	7.35	.00	3.99	.00	1.27	.82	5.16	.57	2.54	.40
04030102	2.59	.00	1.37	.00	1.68	.09	1.50	.17	.50	.00
04030103	.51	.00	.45	.00	.25	.05	.42	.05	.00	.00
04030104	1.50	.00	1.03	.00	1.41	.08	.73	.08	.05	.60
04030105	.86	.00	.85	.00	.92	.14	.43	.05	1.57	2.55
04030106	.08	.00	.04	.00	.05	.01	.01	.00	.00	.00
04030108	.39	.00	.67	.00	.93	.11	.33	.04	.00	.00
04030201	4.42	.00	2.98	.00	29.74	.29	1.57	.17	5.50	.36
04030202	10.95	.00	5.26	.00	67.52	1.44	3.26	.36	3.67	14.29
04030203	6.00	21.15	1.52	.00	.48	.11	1.28	.14	.00	.00
04030204	19.68	2.77	1.57	.00	.55	.30	1.98	.22	.00	.04
04040002	.60	.00	2.71	.00	2.74	.21	.16	.02	.38	1.00
04040003	13.86	.00	5.02	.00	1.45	.25	1.53	.17	.00	.00
04060200	.00	219.01	.00	.00	.00	.00	.00	.00	.00	1.84
07030001	.75	.00	.98	.00	1.11	.04	.38	.04	.48	1.50
07030002	.50	.00	.67	.00	2.49	.02	.36	.04	.36	.36
07030005	7.43	.00	2.73	.00	1.90	.23	1.88	.21	4.83	2.23
07040001	1.26	.00	.71	.00	.32	.04	.85	.09	.00	.00
07040003	.86	.00	.53	.00	2.99	.12	1.28	.14	.00	.00
07040005	1.99	.00	.56	.00	4.70	.11	1.18	.13	.00	.00
07040006	17.06	.00	1.74	.00	1.60	.14	.84	.09	1.55	.04
07040007	2.59	.00	2.21	.00	5.76	.54	3.36	.37	.00	.00
07050001	.26	.00	1.35	.00	9.66	.34	1.69	.19	.00	.00
07050002	1.40	.00	.58	.00	1.70	.16	.26	.03	.50	5.00
07050003	.31	.00	.33	.00	.60	.04	.16	.02	.00	.00
07050004	.19	.00	.37	.00	.29	.13	.40	.04	.00	.00
07050005	14.44	.00	2.02	.00	12.74	.54	2.91	.32	.00	.04
07050006	2.22	.00	1.25	.00	2.15	.23	1.35	.15	.00	.00
07050007	6.75	.00	2.28	.00	27.61	.57	2.56	.28	.39	.04
07060001	2.36	.00	.87	.00	.17	.25	1.00	.11	1.40	.04
07060003	2.34	0.00	0.55	0.00	0.17	0.14	2.05	0.23	0.00	0.00

Appendix 2. Overall water use by category and by subbasin in Wisconsin, 2005.

[Mgal/d, million gallons per day; gWh, gigawatthour(s) of energy produced; thermoelectric, thermoelectric power generation]

	WITHDRAWALS, in Mgal/d										
	Industrial		**Commercial**		**Thermoelectric**		**Mining**		**Total water use**		
Subbasin 8-digit hydrologic unit code	**Ground water**	**Surface water**	**Ground water**	**Surface water**	**Ground water**	**Surface water**	**Ground water**	**Surface water**	**Total ground water**	**Total surface water**	**Total**
04010201	0.00	0.06	0.00	0.00	0.00	0.00	0.01	0.01	0.09	0.07	0.16
04010301	.02	.96	.08	.00	.00	.00	.54	.07	6.09	1.07	7.16
04010302	.04	1.11	.03	.00	.00	.00	.21	.02	1.11	1.27	2.38
04020101	.00	.00	.00	.00	.00	.00	.00	.00	.08	0.00	0.08
04020102	.00	.00	.00	.00	.00	.44	.00	.00	.05	.44	.49
04020300	.00	.00	.00	.00	.00	50.56	.00	.00	.00	66.24	66.24
04030101	2.21	18.14	.48	.00	1.02	.00	.89	.81	24.91	20.74	45.65
04030102	.64	6.11	.22	.00	.01	.00	.20	.19	8.71	6.56	15.27
04030103	.40	8.64	.08	.00	.00	.00	.23	.21	2.34	8.95	11.29
04030104	.23	2.04	.08	.00	.00	.00	.15	.14	5.18	2.94	8.12
04030105	.76	4.58	.03	.00	.00	1.31	.08	.07	5.50	8.70	14.20
04030106	.00	.00	.00	.00	.00	.00	.01	.01	.19	.02	0.21
04030108	.72	4.16	.02	.00	.00	24.87	.08	.07	3.14	29.25	32.39
04030201	3.35	15.91	.65	.00	.00	.00	.89	.80	49.10	17.53	66.63
04030202	6.87	48.48	.60	.00	.00	.00	.94	.68	99.07	65.25	164.32
04030203	1.63	10.18	.07	.00	.00	8.29	.10	.09	11.08	39.96	51.04
04030204	2.85	60.74	.36	.00	.00	448.42	.31	.27	27.30	512.76	540.06
04040002	1.90	4.45	.35	.00	.00	.00	.66	.60	9.50	6.28	15.78
04040003	3.10	4.69	.82	.00	.00	167.42	.83	.35	26.61	172.88	199.49
04060200	.00	.00	.00	.00	.00	4,531.15	.00	.00	.00	4,752.00	4,752.00
07030001	.12	.43	.06	.00	.00	.00	.22	.12	4.10	2.13	6.23
07030002	.21	.11	.17	.00	.00	.00	.15	.03	4.91	.56	5.48
07030005	2.53	.06	.16	.00	.00	.82	.47	.42	21.93	3.97	25.90
07040001	.22	.25	.02	.00	.00	.00	.10	.09	3.48	.47	3.95
07040003	.32	.27	.03	.00	.66	532.50	.04	.02	6.71	533.05	539.76
07040005	.19	.00	.02	.00	.00	.00	.13	.04	8.77	.28	9.05
07040006	3.06	.00	.57	.00	.42	42.16	.65	.59	27.49	43.02	70.51
07040007	1.52	19.05	.30	.00	.00	.00	.84	.52	16.58	20.48	37.06
07050001	1.17	1.59	.84	.00	.00	.00	.29	.25	15.26	2.37	17.63
07050002	.21	1.03	.12	.00	.00	3.74	.05	.05	4.82	10.01	14.83
07050003	.34	3.08	.03	.00	.00	.00	.02	.02	1.79	3.16	4.95
07050004	.23	2.41	.00	.00	.00	.00	.13	.12	1.61	2.70	4.31
07050005	1.06	4.69	.09	.00	.00	.00	.44	.39	33.70	5.98	39.68
07050006	.23	2.17	.05	.00	.00	.00	.15	.13	7.40	2.68	10.08
07050007	2.58	.21	.13	.00	.00	.00	.31	.07	42.61	1.17	43.78
07060001	.81	.00	.14	.00	.15	209.79	.16	.14	7.06	210.33	217.39
07060003	0.20	0.00	0.01	0.00	0.04	255.94	0.09	0.09	5.45	256.40	261.85

Appendix 2. Overall water use by category and by subbasin in Wisconsin, 2005—Continued.

[Mgal/d, million gallons per day; gWh, gigawatthour(s) of energy produced; thermoelectric, thermoelectric power generation]

Subbasin 8-digit hydrologic unit code	WITHDRAWALS, in Mgal/d									
	Public supply		Domestic		Irrigation		Livestock		Aquaculture	
	Ground water	Surface water	Ground water	Surface water	Ground water	Surface water	Ground water	Surface water	Ground water	Surface water
07060005	.48	.00	.15	.00	.03	.05	.63	.07	.00	.00
07070001	2.64	.00	1.83	.00	3.56	.25	.16	.02	1.70	1.08
07070002	15.29	.00	3.05	.00	16.81	3.04	3.06	.34	1.10	.00
07070003	21.03	.00	4.69	.00	120.34	.91	2.83	.31	.48	.11
07070004	5.58	.00	1.28	.00	3.42	.12	.86	.10	.33	.04
07070005	5.23	.00	3.53	.00	8.49	1.17	4.02	.45	.03	.00
07070006	.42	.00	.74	.00	.76	.33	1.12	.12	.00	.00
07090001	15.49	.00	5.35	.00	7.66	.20	3.80	.42	2.93	.00
07090002	76.57	.00	7.36	.00	21.17	.40	2.78	.31	2.94	.00
07090003	3.79	.00	1.22	.00	6.39	.22	2.75	.31	.24	.00
07090004	2.47	.00	1.86	.00	6.89	.09	1.53	.17	.00	.00
07090005	.00	.00	.05	.00	.32	.00	.02	.00	.00	.00
07090006	.49	.00	.12	.00	.10	.02	.04	.00	1.11	.00
07120004	.82	.00	1.21	.00	.41	.09	.09	.01	.00	.00
07120006	23.11	.00	7.06	.00	4.64	.63	.70	.08	.00	.00
Total	305.56	246.94	87.70	.00	386.56	15.21	65.56	7.26	38.48	43.19

Appendix 2. Overall water use by category and by subbasin in Wisconsin, 2005—Continued.

[Mgal/d, million gallons per day; gWh, gigawatthour(s) of energy produced; thermoelectric, thermoelectric power generation]

| Subbasin 8-digit hydrologic unit code | WITHDRAWALS, in Mgal/d | | | | | | | | | | |
| | Industrial | | Commercial | | Thermoelectric | | Mining | | Total water use | | |
	Ground water	Surface water	Ground water	Surface water	Ground water	Surface water	Ground water	Surface water	Total ground water	Total surface water	Total
07060005	.02	.00	.01	.00	.00	.00	.02	.02	1.34	.14	1.48
07070001	.43	11.06	.09	.00	.00	17.22	.10	.09	10.51	29.72	40.23
07070002	1.90	51.26	.17	.00	.45	293.63	.68	.58	42.51	348.85	391.36
07070003	8.21	107.80	.77	.00	.50	25.03	1.04	.59	159.89	134.75	294.64
07070004	.66	.00	.07	.00	.00	.00	.34	.30	12.54	.56	13.10
07070005	2.19	.10	.29	.00	.00	.00	.41	.66	24.19	2.38	26.57
07070006	.29	.00	.07	.00	.00	.00	.05	.05	3.45	0.50	3.95
07090001	6.30	.24	.38	.00	.00	1.97	.95	.74	42.86	3.57	46.42
07090002	7.29	.36	.87	.00	.12	279.28	1.17	1.87	120.27	282.22	402.49
07090003	.65	.02	.15	.00	.00	.00	.07	.12	15.26	.67	15.93
07090004	1.45	.10	.15	.00	.00	.00	.09	.37	14.44	.73	15.17
07090005	.06	.00	.01	.00	.00	.00	.00	.00	.46	.00	.46
07090006	.04	.00	.03	.00	.00	.00	.07	0.06	2.00	.08	2.08
07120004	.05	.96	.06	.00	.00	.00	.12	.10	2.76	1.16	3.92
07120006	1.65	2.26	.91	.00	.00	.00	2.11	1.91	40.18	4.88	45.06
Total	7.91	399.76	1.64	.00	3.37	6,894.54	17.60	14.93	986.38	7,621.83	8,608.21

Appendix 3. Water use for thermoelectric-power generation in Wisconsin, by subbasin, 2005.

[Mgal/d, million gallons per day; gWh, gigawatthour(s) of energy produced]

Subbasin 8-digit hydrologic unit code	Ground-water withdrawal (Mgal/d)	Surface-water withdrawal (Mgal/d)	Total withdrawal (Mgal/d)	Power generated (gWh)	Number of facilities accounted for using ground water	Number of facilities accounted for using surface water
04010201	0.00	0.00	0.00	0.00	0	0
04010301	.00	.00	.00	.00	0	0
04010302	.00	.00	.00	.00	0	0
04020101	.00	.00	.00	.00	0	0
04020102	.00	.44	.44	2.96	0	1
04020300	.00	50.56	50.56	337.08	0	1
04030101	1.02	.00	1.02	102.05	1	0
04030102	.01	.00	.01	1.13	1	0
04030103	.00	.00	.00	.00	0	0
04030104	.00	.00	.00	.00	0	0
04030105	.00	1.31	1.31	8.76	0	1
04030106	.00	.00	.00	.00	0	0
04030108	.00	24.87	24.87	234.61	0	1
04030201	.00	.00	.00	.00	0	0
04030202	.00	.00	.00	.00	0	0
04030203	.00	8.29	8.29	55.24	0	2
04030204	.00	448.42	448.42	3,123.92	0	7
04040002	.00	.00	.00	.00	0	0
04040003	.00	167.42	167.42	1,554.58	0	4
04060200	.00	4,531.15	4,531.15	30,147.38	0	7
07030001	.00	.00	.00	.00	0	0
07030002	.00	.00	.00	.00	0	0
07030005	.00	.82	.82	5.48	0	1
07040001	.00	.00	.00	.00	0	0
07040003	.66	532.50	533.16	3,710.27	1	2
07040005	.00	.00	.00	.00	0	0
07040006	.42	42.16	42.58	77.10	1	3
07040007	.00	.00	.00	.00	0	0
07050001	.00	.00	.00	.00	0	0
07050002	.00	3.74	3.74	24.97	0	1
07050003	.00	.00	.00	.00	0	0
07050004	.00	.00	.00	.00	0	0
07050005	.00	.00	.00	.00	0	0
07050006	.00	.00	.00	.00	0	0
07050007	.00	.00	.00	.00	0	0
07060001	.15	209.79	209.94	2540.59	1	1
07060003	.04	255.94	255.98	1,470.08	1	2
07060005	.00	.00	.00	.00	0	0
07070001	.00	17.22	17.22	114.78	0	2
07070002	.45	293.63	294.08	4,496.50	1	8

Appendix 3. Water use for thermoelectric-power generation in Wisconsin, by subbasin, 2005—Continued.

[Mgal/d, million gallons per day; gWh, gigawatthour(s) of energy produced]

Subbasin 8-digit hydrologic unit code	Ground-water withdrawal (Mgal/d)	Surface-water withdrawal (Mgal/d)	Total withdrawal (Mgal/d)	Power generated (gWh)	Number of facilities accounted for using ground water	Number of facilities accounted for using surface water
07070003	0.50	25.03	25.53	6,745.41	1	3
07070004	.00	.00	.00	.00	0	0
07070005	.00	.00	.00	.00	0	0
07070006	.00	.00	.00	.00	0	0
07090001	.00	1.97	1.97	13.14	0	1
07090002	.12	279.28	279.40	1,795.46	1	8
07090003	.00	.00	.00	.00	0	0
07090004	.00	.00	.00	.00	0	0
07090005	.00	.00	.00	.00	0	0
07090006	.00	.00	.00	.00	0	0
07120004	.00	.00	.00	.00	0	0
07120006	.00	.00	.00	.00	0	0
Total	3.37	6,894.55	6,897.92	56,561.49	11	56

Appendix 4. Public-supply withdrawals, number of facilities, and per-capita use in Wisconsin, by subbasin, 2005.

[Population, in 1000s of persons; withdrawals, in million gallons per day (Mgal/d); per-capita use, in gallons per day per person (gal/d/person)]

Subbasin 8-digit hydrologic unit code	Number of public-supply facilities[a]	Public-supply withdrawal[b] (Mgal/d)	Population served ground water	Population served surface water	Public-supply per capita (gal/d/person)
04010201	2	0.01	0.40	13.98	0.7
04010301	6	.37	3.58	22.58	14.1
04010302	6	.27	2.12	1.80	68.9
04020101	0	.00	.00	0.00	.0
04020102	1	.00	.00	.00	.0
04020300	0	4.01	.00	.00	.0
04030101	31	7.35	48.91	115.36	44.7
04030102	8	2.59	19.11	.00	135.5
04030103	3	.51	5.83	.00	87.5
04030104	7	1.50	11.04	.00	135.9
04030105	6	.86	6.38	11.75	47.4
04030106	1	.08	1.81	.00	44.2
04030108	3	.39	3.27	.00	119.3
04030201	18	4.42	37.55	63.98	43.5
04030202	33	10.95	67.51	.00	162.2
04030203	7	27.15	51.34	3.30	496.9
04030204	22	22.45	152.11	245.63	56.4
04040002	16	.60	7.26	338.78	1.7
04040003	21	13.86	128.44	803.24	14.9
04060200	0	219.01	.00	.00	.0

Appendix 4. Public-supply withdrawals, number of facilities, and per-capita use in Wisconsin, by subbasin, 2005 —Continued.

[Population, in 1000s of persons; withdrawals, in million gallons per day (Mgal/d); per-capita use, in gallons per day per person (gal/d/person)]

Subbasin 8-digit hydrologic unit code	Number of public-supply facilities[a]	Public-supply withdrawal[b] (Mgal/d)	Population served ground water	Population served surface water	Public-supply per capita (gal/d/person)
07030001	5	0.75	5.79	0.00	129.5
07030002	3	.50	2.95	.00	169.5
07030005	23	7.43	60.29	.49	122.2
07040001	7	1.26	12.49	.00	100.9
07040003	8	.86	8.80	.00	97.7
07040005	10	1.99	8.57	.00	232.2
07040006	11	17.06	92.19	.00	185.1
07040007	16	2.59	21.08	.00	122.9
07050001	7	.26	2.02	.00	128.7
07050002	4	1.40	7.86	.00	178.1
07050003	2	.31	1.95	.00	159.0
07050004	5	.19	1.33	.00	142.9
07050005	15	14.44	94.23	.00	153.2
07050006	7	2.22	15.45	.00	143.7
07050007	17	6.75	39.66	.00	170.2
07060001	10	2.36	15.49	.00	152.4
07060003	15	2.34	22.18	.00	105.5
07060005	8	.48	6.44	.00	74.5
07070001	7	2.64	17.08	.00	154.6
07070002	19	15.29	103.67	.00	147.5
07070003	35	21.03	117.07	.00	179.6
07070004	15	5.58	28.24	.00	197.6
07070005	34	5.23	44.88	.00	116.5
07070006	10	.42	5.84	.00	71.9
07090001	28	15.49	128.34	.00	120.7
07090002	44	76.57	542.18	.00	141.2
07090003	19	3.79	17.64	.00	214.9
07090004	11	2.47	36.43	.00	67.8
07090005	0	.00	.00	.00	0.0
07090006	1	.49	2.62	.00	187.0
07120004	3	.82	6.11	.04	133.3
07120006	25	23.11	206.25	40.18	93.8

[a] A facility is counted where the water distribution network resides on land; therefore, those hydrologic units listed with zero facilities but with withdrawals were counted in an adjacent land-based hydrologic unit.

[b] The amount of water withdrawn for public supply is assigned to where the withdrawal occurs (originates from) not to where it was used.

www.ingramcontent.com/pod-product-compliance
Lightning Source LLC
Chambersburg PA
CBHW080431290526
45791CB00008BA/2458